let's get
practical

Cover Design:	Yamilca Rodriguez, Zachary L. Houghton, Luke Houghton
Interior Design:	Zachary L. Houghton
Interior Illustrations:	Sage Toomey
Interior Layout:	Olivier Darbonville

Published by st. john's press
www.stjohnspress.com

For general information and special discounts on bulk purchases, please email info@stjohnspress.com or visit www.stjohnspress.com.

LIBRARY OF CONGRESS CATALOGING-IN-PUBLICATION DATA
Thon, Bjørn Arild

Let's Get Practical
Igniting Human Energy to Drive the Circular Economy Transition

Library of Congress Control Number (LCCN): 2024903235
Hardback ISBN: 978-1-955027-15-1
Paperback ISBN: 978-1-955027-16-8
E-book ISBN: 978-1-955027-13-7
Audiobook ISBN: 978-1-955027-17-5

First edition: March 2024

Printed and bound in the United States of America.

Two percent of proceeds from the sale of the book will go to the Nexus Council, a nonprofit 501(c)(3) public charity. The Nexus Council's mission is to bridge voices and drive solutions to discover common ground in a divided society in order to support a more sustainable, free, and abundant world.

let's get practical

Igniting Human Energy to Drive the Circular Economy Transition

Bjørn Arild Thon

with J.J. Brown, Torund Bryhn, and Ian Peterman

let's get

practical

Igniting Human Energy to Drive
the Circular Economy Transition

dedication

This book is dedicated to all the precious living beings on planet Earth.

My hope is that this book serves as a reminder of how we are all connected and that the potential for goodness exists in every one of us. In today's world, hatred and shame creates too many divisions. May we find inspiration from these pages and from the interconnected natural world around us to bridge these divisions and make our world a better place for all.

contents

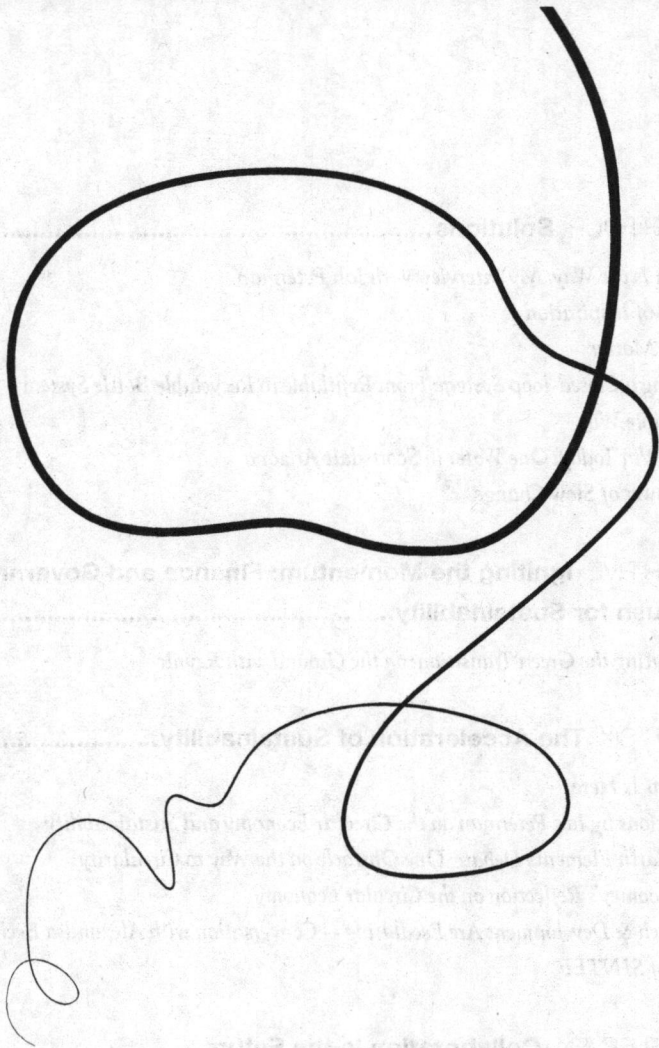

introduction

IMAGINE YOU ARE SWIMMING in the Pacific Ocean, the wide-open waters stretching out before you. With every kick, you take yourself further into the blue, feeling the power of nature, along with a sense of calm that comes with being immersed.

Suddenly, you feel something odd brush on your shoulder, and you stop mid-stroke. Pieces of plastic waste are floating all around you. Unfortunately, this isn't the first time you have encountered this kind of pollution. You sigh and begin to collect the debris.

This swimmer was Benoit Lecomte, and his experience of encountering trash in the oceans inspired him to shift his focus from endurance swimming to addressing the global problem of the tremendous amounts of trash in our oceans.

In 2018, Lecomte attempted to swim across the Pacific Ocean in order to highlight the problem of marine plastic pollution. As he swam, Benoît collected plastic every five minutes, revealing the heartbreaking extent of pollution in the open sea, far from any landmass. More important than Benoit's personal achievement in endurance was the attention he drew to this global issue. He wasn't the first person to discover ocean pollution or to shine a light on it, but this endurance swimmer saw a problem and made the decision to become part of the solution; he found his own green pivot. He did not need to abandon his chosen career to begin supporting the planet. He integrated his new mindset into the life he was leading. He asked himself, *What can I do?* And then he did it.

$$\Big[\text{He asked himself "What can I do?"} \\ \text{And then he did it.} \Big]$$

Our planet consists of seventy percent water. We are the shining blue planet in the solar system. Our survival depends on the health of that water. Because the ocean is as yet largely unexplored, we have much to learn about it—how it works and what the effects of our choices are on it.

My green pivot

Back when I was 18, I enlisted in the US Navy. After boot camp and training, I was stationed on the USS Coral Sea, an aircraft carrier that functioned as a floating city with a crew of nearly 5,000. Looking back, one of the things that struck me about life on the carrier was the amount of waste we produced and the solution we had for treating it. Every week, we would dump our garbage overboard, leaving a trail of trash in the ocean.

I'm sorry to admit that it was mostly in hindsight that I realized the magnitude of the impact we were having on the ocean. I began to have a growing awareness that we could do better.

My *green* pivot led me to ask, "What can I do?"
Answering that question throughout my life has helped me to forge my own green path. No one person can do it all, but the more people who ask themselves that question and act on it, the better things can be for all of us.

My *green pivot* led me down a lifelong path in the recycling industry, seeking ways to enhance our stewardship of resources. Since 2014 I have served as CEO at RENAS, Norway's foremost waste electronic and electrical equipment (WEEE Directive) compliance scheme.

RENAS became the answer to Norway's Minister of Environmental

Affairs Thorbjørn Berntsen's challenge to the nation's electric and electronic industries to embrace accountability and find sustainable solutions for the removal and proper disposal of hazardous substances and recycling of materials left over from industrial processes. In response to this approach to "end-of-life" treatment, a collective of industry leaders (Norsk Industri & Norsk Elektroforeningen) joined forces and established RENAS AS in 1997. The overarching vision was clear: to remove hazardous substances in a secure matter and convert waste into a valuable resource, while advocating an accountable approach that safeguards the environment.

My work at RENAS has extended beyond Norway's borders, allowing me to engage in dialogues and collaborations with global leaders, corporations, and citizens. Together, we are reimagining the way we approach our practices and responsibilities on adopting the principles of the circular economy.

You might ask at this point, "What is the circular economy?" "What does this have to do with me?"

A Circular Economy seeks to extract the maximum value from materials while in use and then recover, reuse, and repurpose these materials at the end of each products life cycle.

The circular economy is the idea of learning from nature and adopting a system that mimics nature.

Nature exchanges energy and value with no waste.

Nature's cycles are designed such that energy is broken down and reused. As you may have observed, human actions are currently disrupting the natural cycles of the environment. This disruption comes from the creation of waste that does not integrate into the natural cycle of life. Instead, it remains stagnant and unproductive.

Janez Potočnik, a Slovenian economist and a leading figure in the circular economy, remarked, "The circular economy is the oldest concept on Earth: in nature nothing is lost, and everything has its purpose."[1]

The principal of the *circular economy* is to adopt and design a system where materials never become waste and nature is regenerated. [2]

In nature, fallen leaves break down to fertilize the ground. The body of an animal becomes food for another, which then becomes food for yet another. Everything is replenished.

The circular economy aims to minimize waste and pollution by maximizing the use of resources. It involves reducing, reusing, and recycling resources to create a closed-loop system where value is never lost. The circular economy focuses on designing products and processes with sustainability in mind, so they can be reshaped, repaired, or recycled.

What's the opposite of a circular economy?

A linear economy is an economic system where products are designed, produced, used, and then thrown away, often without reuse or recycling, relying heavily on continuously consuming new raw materials. Today we primarily operate within a linear economic framework. This approach requires an ongoing consumption of fresh raw materials, presenting great challenges for sustainable resource management and long-term profitability, and poses a detriment to the health of our planet.

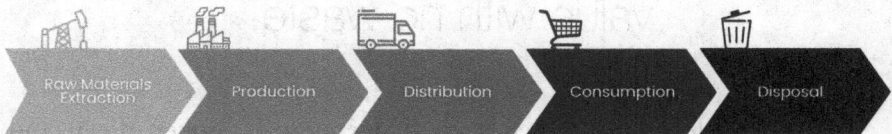

Raw Materials Extraction → Production → Distribution → Consumption → Disposal

Our Current Model: The Linear Model

What can you do?

The purpose of this book is to inspire your own *green pivot* and encourage you and your organization to be catalysts for change within your community. I encourage you to be the change that propels society, as a whole, toward a circular economy and a sustainable future. Throughout these pages, we'll explore the core concepts of the circular economy, clarifying its true nature and dispelling misconceptions. By adopting a nature-centric perspective, we can complement governmental regulations with effective and lasting change.

What is a green pivot?

During the COVID-19 pandemic, the word "pivot" was on everyone's lips, transforming from a term primarily reserved for business strategies into a universally understood concept. It became a buzzword for adaptation as individuals and organizations worldwide were required to switch gears and adjust their courses.

In sailing, tacking involves changing the direction of a boat by positioning the position of the sail or rudder. It's a strategic maneuver to navigate changing winds or adjust the course.

Similarly, in life, to tack means to make a deliberate change in your approach or perspective to adapt to new circumstances or goals. Just as a sailor adjusts their boat's sails to catch the wind, a personal tack might involve adjusting your actions to catch opportunities or align with your aspirations. It's about being flexible, responsive, and innovative, whether on the water or in your journey through life.

While I acknowledge the value of a full change in course , most people do not have a single 180-degree reversal, but rather slowly change over time.

For me, a green pivot signifies more than just changing habits; it's a shift in mindset toward adopting the principles of the circular economy. It involves embracing sustainable choices, rethinking consumption patterns, and considering the environmental impact of my actions. It's a conscious effort to align my values with actions that contribute to a healthier planet.

> "A Green Pivot signifies more than changing habits; it's a shift in mindset towards adopting the principles of the circular economy."

What is your green pivot?

It is more than a little tempting as a passionate educator who cares deeply about our Earth to begin telling you what you should do to adopt a more nature-centered mindset and contribute to a more sustainable or circular lifestyle, but only you can decide your own path and the scale of the contribution that works for you. **There is greater potential in a thousand different small contributions than in one thousand people all doing the same thing and working on the same solution.**

About this book

Although not an author by trade, I reluctantly agreed to write this book on the circular economy. I declined multiple times and tried to recruit others to write the book. It was not until 2022 that I finally agreed, because no one had stepped up. My publisher reminded me that my military background provided the necessary training and endurance. She jokingly noted that I could have been a Navy SEAL if I were an American citizen. Why not apply my training to a more peaceful, fruitful end? So, I view this writing challenge as an extension and evolution of my green journey.

Why I wrote this book

Having worked in the recycling business for two decades, I have seen my share of scare tactics used by activists and government groups to effect change. When activists use scare tactics to address environmental concerns such tactics can cause many to ignore and even suppress the goodwill humans already carry in their hearts and minds toward the environment.

Per Espen Stoknes, an economist, psychologist, professor, and author of *What We Think About When We Try Not to Think About Global Warming*, stated that to create engagement for the public to care about climate change we must move away from the language of doom, because it desensitizes people to efforts to improve their ways. He said, "Climate change is usually framed as a looming disaster, bringing losses, cost, and sacrifice. That makes us fearful. But after the first fear is gone, my brain soon wants to avoid this topic altogether."

Rather than inspire humans to action, the scare tactics turn environmental problems into monsters too large to be relatable to individuals and even members of the industry. The statistics and numbers we hear about the climate are so large it is hard for everyday people to connect and feel any responsibility for the issue.

> Hope and faith are more sustainable motivations than fear, but too much fear kills all hope.

Let's get beyond climate fear and focus on steps we can take right now to live in harmony with nature. Blaming others for the current state of our environment is not productive. We need to recognize that we all play a role in the demand for energy and other resources, and work together to find solutions that are inclusive of all industries. We should all be asking ourselves, "What am I going to do about it?"

Rather than solely focusing on the symptoms of environmental degradation, we need to understand the root causes of these issues. This will allow us to think creatively and to consider new approaches that prioritize the health and well-being of the planet.

> "Let's get beyond climate fear and focus on steps we can take right now to live in harmony with nature. "

In the end, our goal is to establish a strong, healthy, and sustainable Earth that can support future generations. This requires us to take a step back, think critically, and be open to new ideas and perspectives.

How?

We go back to nature.

"Let's Get Practical" is a book about going back to our natural roots. It is about looking to nature and the principles we have lived by for the whole of human history, but enhancing them with the blessings of modern knowledge and advancement. At the core of our actions and beliefs lies a profound connection to nature and our origins. Our love for fellow humans, animals, and the natural world drives us to acknowledge the essential role that green trees, bees, and clean water play in sustaining us.

I like to call it the nature-based mindset.

A **nature-based mindset** is a holistic approach that recognizes the interdependence of all living things and their ecosystems. It emphasizes the importance of working with nature rather than against it and seeks to restore and regenerate natural systems. This mindset is grounded in the understanding that humans are part of nature and that our actions impact the natural world around us. It is possible for human life and even human growth to thrive along with nature.

We understand that every aspect, every nook, and cranny of nature is a part of an interconnected circle of life, and it is our duty to work toward its preservation. By recognizing our dependence on nature and embracing a nature-based mindset, we can begin to prioritize the protection and conservation of our environment and its resources.

This change in mindset can help businesses recognize that their success is not only tied to financial gain but also to their impact on the environment and society as a whole. By embracing a nature-based approach, businesses can make decisions that promote sustainability and environmental stewardship, while also driving innovation and growth. This long-term perspective can produce long-term, perpetual benefits for the company and the planet.

Look to the farmers

For me, practicality and the nature-based mindset mirror the ways of farmers and rural communities. Being practical means using experience, wisdom, and logic to solve problems efficiently. It is about finding simple solutions to complex challenges. For the farmers, this means dealing with a wide range of challenges related to biology, technology, hardware, and software, often simultaneously. With limited time and resources, they must rely on what they have learned from their hands-on experience to fix equipment, mend fences, and address any other issues that arise with crops or livestock.

Simply stated, by adopting the mindset of practicality and nature-based mindset, we can strive for a more intentional and sustainable approach to our creative pursuits.

By embracing a circular mindset, we can create innovative solutions grounded in common sense. The good news is that practical solutions exist now, and the path to a circular economy is already being paved around the globe with proven methods just waiting to be adopted as part of as our own personal green pivot journey. As we each experience green pivots and ask ourselves what we can do, we will be drawn to the practices that work best for us or we may discover our own brand-new solutions.

Brief overview

The book will begin with an overview of the circular economy and then reflect on the origins of our consumer-driven society to uncover a sense of clarity on how to move forward. It is in knowing our history that we can change direction. I also show nature's ability to restore balance despite past setbacks. This serves as a reminder of our capacity for transformative change.

In this book, you will find practical solutions, highlighting the significance of a holistic approach, share solutions that have proven effective in the past. You will discover the crucial role of initial decisions, such as design, the importance of words, and the triple win.

The final chapters move to our current circumstances, showcasing the potential for individual impact in driving change. You'll find practical guidance on personal actions that can foster transformation.

Throughout the process of crafting this book, I've engaged in enlightening discussions with leaders who have embraced the principles of a circular economy. Their diverse and innovative contributions underscore the momentum of this transformative movement.

Clarification

I want to clarify that this book is not about debating the legitimacy or extent of impact of climate change. That is a term I personally avoid using, because it tends to overshadow so many other unrelated environmental issues that are also important to us and our everyday lives. I would also like to avoid fear-based arguments, which ignore and even diminish the goodwill humans already carry in their hearts and minds toward the environment.

I want to inspire you and your organization to reflect on your green pivot and to regularly consider the following questions about ways you can help:

What can you do?

What habits can you adopt?

What message can you send?

How can your organization adopt more circular practices?

Who is this book for?

This book is intended for a diverse range of readers who share a common concern for our planet and agree that the way we currently are moving forward is not the answer. The book is intended to welcome newcomers willing to explore the environmental challenges we face as well as experts seeking fresh perspectives to inform their work in sustainability and conservation. Through its pages, I aim to promote critical and creative ideas to address our environmental challenges and provide valuable insights for both large and small changes that will shape the future.

We all leave a legacy

We all contribute how we can when we can. And sometimes simple is best; it is the intention behind the action that is important, to be part of something bigger, something good.

When you choose to "make a difference" or "make a change" over the long term, you must identify, **"What's in it for me?"** The driving motivation behind what you, or anyone, is doing must be rooted in a core value or motive. That basis makes the difference between a short-term change and a long-term solution. Band-aids won't cut it here. If we are trying to make behavioral, structural, and societal changes; they must come from a place of truth and align with our core values.

The Earth's ability to fix and regenerate itself is amazing. Our unrestrained consumerism might not have been a problem for its ecosystems when there were just two, three, and four billion people, but when we pass eight billion, racing toward ten and twelve billion, it becomes clear that we are not on a viable path for sustainable resource management.

We received this planet, this invaluable gift, as a legacy from our ancestors. What legacy will we leave for our descendants? As we explore and discuss problems and possible solutions throughout this book, continue to ask yourself these questions:

"What's in it for me today?"

"What's in it for me over five years?"

"What's in it for me over my lifetime?"

"What's in it for me through my grandchild's lifetime?"

A legacy should be an aspiration, a way of life worthy of living. Creating a legacy means making a promise to the future and contributing to benefit future generations. It involves imagining how the world will be when you are gone. The choices that you make between now and the day that you depart this world are your legacy.

Embracing the circular economy: a journey of small actions and collective impact

> If you want to go fast, go alone.
> If you want to go far, go together.
> *-African Proverb*

Disclaimer: I'm not trying to put the world on your shoulders.

In a world grappling with environmental challenges and mounting concerns about our planet's future, it's easy to feel overwhelmed by the weight of responsibility. This is the feedback I got from someone who initially read the book, as if the burden of saving the world rested solely on their shoulders.

However, I want to assure you that my intention is far from burdening you with the responsibility of saving the world. Instead, this book aims to inspire you, the individual, to recognize that your actions, whether modest or grand, possess the potential to create a positive and lasting impact on the environment and human prosperity for generations to come.

When reading this book, I invite you to consider the following questions and let them be at the heart of our journey together:

1 Take a moment to reflect on your daily routine. What small changes can you make in your personal life to conserve resources, promote sustainability, and reduce waste?

2 Have you ever considered the environmental impact of your consumer/consumption choices; from the products you buy to the companies you support? How might you align your consumer behavior with your core values?

3 Can you identify one specific environmental issue or challenge that resonates with you personally? How might you take meaningful action to address this issue, even on a small scale, and inspire positive

4 change within your community?

Have you ever felt overwhelmed by the idea of saving the world on your own? And has this led you to create a narrative that it is someone else's job, thus avoiding taking personal action? How does shifting your perspective from individual responsibility to collective action change your outlook?

Starting at the micro level, we will explore how each of us can become better stewards of the environment, understanding that small changes can ripple outward and yield substantial results. We will then turn our focus to the macro perspective, delving into the power of collective action and collaboration to bring about significant, substantial, and profound change.

As we shift toward a more sustainable world, we must keep one critical principle at the forefront of our decision-making: a long-term, seven-generation perspective. This long-term perspective reminds us of the importance of thinking beyond the present and considering the legacy we leave for those who will inherit the world we shape today. These insightful words by Forest James, Chief Executive Officer of EnerTribe, Inc. and Founder of Earthprint Technologies, guide our exploration. Together, we will explore how our actions, whether on an individual or collective level, can contribute to a brighter, more sustainable future—one that considers the well-being of generations yet to come.

In addition to my personal and professional insights into practical sustainable steps forward, I've collaborated with experts to help bring diverse perspectives to the concept of the circular economy.

Torund Bryhn, my strategist, researcher, and voicewriter, has played a crucial role in helping to showcase my perspective and infuse my voice into these pages.

JJ Brown has a focus on policy-oriented matters, offering a nuanced exploration of how regulations and governance can shape the circular economy's future.

Ian Peterman, an expert in Conscious Design, illuminates the intersection of creativity and sustainability, highlighting the importance of thoughtful product design in reducing waste and maximizing value.

Sage Toomey provides a Gen-Z perspective, offering fresh insights and ideas that bridge the generation gap.

Bringing in these esteemed contributors helps to enrich our collective understanding of the circular economy, illustrating that collaboration is at the heart of this transformative movement—something we'll explore in-depth throughout this book. As we journey together, let's embrace the power of collaboration, understanding that true change comes not just from within but from the synergy of diverse voices and expertise.

So, thank you for joining me in discovering the boundless potential of the circular economy and how, together, we can create a world where responsible stewardship of our environment becomes second nature.

chapter one

origins of our dilemmas

How did it all begin?

When did we lose our way?

When did our habits and lifestyle pile up, causing such harm to our planet?

We never intended to find ourselves in this predicament. Yet, as we raced down the fast lane of progress and efficiency, we encountered unexpected dilemmas in our pursuit of sustainability.

Before we look to the future, in this chapter, we take a step back and pause to reflect. How did our grandparents live, and what can we learn from their way of life?

What dilemmas are we facing now as we chase after one-dimensional solutions?

And what were the driving forces that led us to adopt a linear economy?

By looking back and understanding our current state, we gain a clearer perspective on potential solutions. This retrospective exploration is crucial for paving a more sustainable and thoughtful path forward.

We Were Circular Once

WHEN I WAS GROWING UP in the 1970s in Norway, we didn't have a lot. We had all we needed, but items were commonly handed down from one person to another. I used to inherit my older brothers' clothes, skis, and bicycles. We patched our pants and mended our shirts and socks when they got rips or holes. While we didn't have a name for it, since this way of life was just what we knew, it is a perfect example of small ways to practice circular economy principles.

I realize it will be a challenge to become as 'circular' as my grandparents. They hardly ever threw anything away. When they did, rest assured it was because there was nothing left to salvage. If they couldn't fix something themselves, they would go to a repair shop or to someone who knew how to fix that product. Even if they could afford a new item, it would never occur to them to throw something away that still had value.

Things were generally made to last longer, and society was designed for this type of consumer behavior. People had less money, and things were expensive, so they fixed things. Most people had the mindset that products should be kept and cared for in the long term. No one would raise an eyebrow when I came to school in pants that were patched both on the knee and butt and that my brother had used a couple of years earlier. That was the way. There was no expectation of always having new things. It was a simpler life. It was a time when being 'circular' was part of every-day life.

What can we learn from our great-grandparents or grandparents?

Many of our grandparents were kids during or before World War II. They didn't have many of the luxuries we take for granted today, but they had what they needed and what they had they cared for and made it last. Sufficient food was available, but the incredible diversity and surplus of food we enjoy today due to food being shipped from all around the world was not their reality.

What I am saying is that their baseline in time shaped their values, their habits, how they saw things, and how they valued them. For them it was not for the sake of the environment, but because it made practical and financial sense.

After any meal, they would carefully save leftovers for later, and they would use them, not just throw them away after a few days in the fridge. The idea of throwing away food was anathema.

When their radio broke, they took it to the repair shop and had it fixed. Buying a new one just for a minor issue was not an option; frankly, I don't even think it would have occurred to them. Their shoes were taken to the cobbler for new soles, looking better and more comfortable every year. Watches, clocks, televisions, and other products were repaired, not taken to the trash.

Lots of what they depended on and used was even made locally, or at least within the same region, or country. That meant they would have the whole supply chain within reach. There was always someone who could fix things. Things were meant to be fixed. Now, we consider it a luxury to discard the old item and replace with a brand new one, without further thought about the value we are sending to the landfill.

I often think of my own household today compared to their household and how much waste we generate compared to them. They would take out a small plastic bag, or maybe two, per week. Their garbage can was emptied every two weeks and was never full when the "garbageman" came and dumped it in the back of his truck. Even after holidays like Christmas, with all the extras imaginable, there was still room in their bin at the end of the week. In my household, we make it a point to reduce our waste as much as possible, but still we have on average at least a bag per day.

Even with some sincere effort, my family remains much more wasteful than my grandparents were. I am a child of the 1970s, so my consumer pattern is different. Even though I share many of their values of not overspending and trying to preserve

My grandparent's one small bag compared to my family's seven

and repair thingswhen possible, I am also a child of my time and act accordingly, if for nothing else than to fit into society with my family.

Observation: loss of the repair society

For the last twenty years or so, repair shops of all varieties have disappeared. Nobody repairs anything anymore, so there is no market for someone like a radio repairman. If my TV breaks, I cannot find anyone to fix it. If I do, putting all the hassle aside, the repairs will probably cost at least as much as buying a new TV. A few years ago, I purchased a top-of-the-line TV. It had the newest technology and was expected to last me a very long time before I considered upgrading to a new replacement. So, after five years, the TV still worked fine, but the manufacturer simply stopped providing software updates. As a result, it would no longer work as expected. The expert at the store advised me to replace it with a new upgraded model that would handle the new software updates. In the end, I managed to fix the issue through an external device. I still have the TV today, but it was more me being stubborn and not accepting the expert's advice as the solution than having a good product and customer service.

What could be more wasteful than when products requiring minerals from dozens of different mines are designed to fail?

Producers have discovered this method of locking in new sales, but consumers should take a stand and demand something new.

They are forcing my hand. I must buy a new one.

Where is a cobbler when you need one?

I am not saying they don't exist, but have you seen one lately?

Let me know if you have because I haven't seen a cobbler shop for longer than I care to remember. If I need one, it will be so hard to find and probably too impractical and expensive to even consider. Buying new is my only real alternative in today's economy.

Observation: packaging overload

A couple of years ago, my wife and I carried out a small analysis of the contents of our household waste. Ninety percent or more of it was packaging. All types of packaging. We do sort out everything we can that is recyclable, like metals, glass, cardboard, and some plastic, but still, we can't seem to get our trash down to much less than one 5-gallon bag per day, on average. The amount of packaging seems to just get bigger and bigger.

The smallest things are surrounded by excessive packaging, many times just made for marketing purposes. The last time I bought ink for my home printer, the packaging alone filled an entire bag. On top of that the packaging was so impractical and impenetrable that I had to use industrial-grade scissors to get the product out. In the process, I cut myself on the sharp plastic, bleeding all over the place and creating more waste from the materials used to clean and bandage the cut.

I acknowledge that packaging serves the purpose of protecting the product from damage and allowing it to store longer. That is important. But sometimes I can't help but wonder what would happen if manufacturers designed their products to be as durable as their packaging.

Insight: align actions with your values
That may sound difficult and cumbersome, but I've learned it isn't that hard if you start small and just give it time.

Think of this: You see an ad for a new phone coming onto the market, and the company sells you a story that everything will be better if you buy it. You don't really understand the new specs and what it will do differently than the not-so-old phone you already have, but you feel the urge and kind of want to buy that new phone. It's a little expensive, but you have the money now. The itch is there, and you fold, give in, and buy it. The sensation and excitement you feel as you unpack the new phone from its box is wonderful.

The whole buying experience made you feel good, until you realize that your newly acquired item is basically the same as your old one. Now the little voice in your head, that was there at first, but which you successfully managed to suppress until this moment, starts again, becoming louder and louder. You now have spent twice as much money and used up twice the resources for no real increase in value.

When you remember that you have a small pile of old phones in your desk drawer, that little voice is shouting. Now you're starting to think of the chain of events and consequences of your purchase. Because of the money you spent, you realize you will come up short on the planned dinner with your girlfriend, or worse, that the utility bill is due next week. You can turn to your credit card, leaving you in debt for the next twelve months, suffering from usurious interest rates. Now that little voice is screaming in your head. That is what I call cumbersome.

The other scenario is that you see the ad, have the same emotion, and get the same urge, but you let that little voice in your head say its piece. Give it some time and think about whether you really need this new phone. After a while, look at the ad again Admire the beauty of it, the vibrant colors in the pictures that can take you on a journey, the ingenuity and engineering skills it took to make this product, the creativity and artistry of those who wrote the story and took the photos—and then you decide not to buy the phone. Some extra time with your inner voice results in a final decision in line with your core values, needs, and long-term wishes. A win-win situation for all.

Practical action: count to ten or wait before you buy
Remember that your needs and desires are not the same things, and you will always want more than you need. That's human nature, but we need to control our desires and accept that they are not always looking out for our best interests.

Imagine that you are at a buffet and are very hungry. You grab a plate and quickly fill it to the rim with all the options offered. Your eyes move from one food to another; like a glutton, you gorge on the food being served. Back at the table, you start to eat, and it quickly becomes clear that you can't eat most of the food on your plate. Slightly embarrassed, you try to cover your gluttony with a napkin, discreetly pushing the plate aside and hoping the staff will remove it quickly.

This is a classic encounter in which your wants take control over your needs, with unpleasant results. But you learn from your mistake. The next time you are at the buffet, you scan for all the delicious foods you want to have, make a quick plan in your mind, and take a little at a time, serving yourself several times and giving yourself more time to taste and enjoy the wonders of the different dishes.

These decisions are made up of many factors and aspects that are both subliminal and conscious in nature, with some being easier to address and control than others. The universal factor that will have the most impact is time. Give things a little time to mature. Take time to let all the arguments in your head come out and speak their piece. Time for reflection is an undervalued quality in our consumerist society. Try it—you will be amazed at what a few seconds, minutes, or days of fermenting ideas can do for you.

But be warned, there are side effects. Once you start doing this, you will be filled with the sensation of accomplishment, pride, and confidence. You will feel better about yourself and smile more. Your boost in confidence will radiate, influencing others around you toward the same changes. They might start to see you as a thought leader, a guiding star, and someone to look up to and follow.

More than anything, none of these changes or actions will affect your life in a negative way. No matter what habits you want to change, or create, over time you will probably have fewer things to worry about, both physically and mentally, when you're done. There will be less stuff to clutter your garage and closets and a tidier space around you, giving you more time and energy for the things you truly want to do. You will have more of *you*.

Is it possible for us to go back to expecting more value from our products?

This shift in expectations will require us to go back to the drawing board and focus more on the design stage of production, *i.e.*, demand that our products be designed to last longer. If consumers demand longer-term value from their products, I believe producers and designers will respond. I also believe if we, the consumers, expected used products to be reused or re-purposed, both designers and the waste industry would eventually respond to that demand. The result would be a significantly reduced need for new materials, less energy expended, and much less waste produced.

Misaligned Solutions

THE CALL FOR A CIRCULAR ECONOMY simply arises from the pursuit of a better world and an enhanced quality of life.

Clean water, breathable air, and a nurturing environment are vital to our well-being.

Pollution, deforestation, and habitat loss continue to loom large.

Even amidst the progress we make, a scarcity of rare materials threatens these advances. Primary resources that power our technology and economies endanger the natural environment around us, our wellbeing, and the wellbeing of those who come after us.

I had the privilege of meeting with French journalist, author, and documentary maker Guillaume Pitron, a specialist in the geopolitics of raw materials at the WEEE Forum's Extended Producer Responsibility (EPR) Grand Challenge conference in Brussels in December 2022. The WEEE forum is the world's biggest multi-national collaboration concerning the responsibilities of e-waste producers. They manage the collection and treatment of electrical equipment and electronic waste.

Pitron told me that transitioning to a low-carbon economy brings its own set of dilemmas. We would need to extract and use rare metals and minerals required for major components of our most advanced renewable energy technologies.

This is where a paradox arises: there will be no energy transition without rare earth metals and minerals, yet these resources are not renewables and take a lot of energy to produce. The IEA (International Energy Agency) stated that by 2040 we will need forty-two times more lithium than in 2020 (based on current and projected demand). For graphite and cobalt, the need will be somewhere near twenty times more than in 2020.[3]

The paradox: renewable energy requires nonrenewable resources

Pitron's travels revealed the dark and devastating consequences that mining and processing rare earths and critical minerals has on nature when the extraction occurs in regions with lax regulatory protections. In fact, there is a dirty side to *clean technologies*: the nations with the laxest mining regulations are using their control of resources as a geopolitical game to enhance their global position. Bringing extractive activity for critical minerals back home will not only allow these minerals to be extracted more responsibly, but it will also increase our economic security as we can have closer supervision and management of the process. Friendly allied nations such as the U.S., Canada, Australia and others have an abundance of the critical minerals required by advanced renewable technologies.

How do we make clean technologies in a way that gathers and uses resources in a sustainable and practical way?

I believe we should take off the blinders and address each solution for its true impact and profitability and avoid *greenwashing* technologies. Just because it's green doesn't mean it's clean. We need to separate growth from raw materials by transforming the way we produce and use goods, as well as how we supply raw materials.

Dilemmas in Research

ALEXANDRA BECH GJØRV, the CEO of SINTEF, one of Europe's largest research institutions, admits in the 2022 annual report, "We also face dilemmas where our research may contribute positively to one of the UN Sustainability Development Goals, but risks having an adverse impact on sustainability elsewhere. Therefore, we often need to reflect on the impact our activities have from an ethical point of view and consider which solutions and technologies we should promote."[4]

> "The assessment is, if something is a dilemma, it means that the answers are not a given."
> *-Alexandra Bech Gjorv, CEO, SINTEF*

"SINTEF is deeply committed to addressing these dilemmas and has established corporate initiatives in various areas to actively seek collaborations with institutions that have complementary knowledge," states Gjørv. Some examples are:

Biodiversity and mineral needs. As our society moves into the green transition, more metals and minerals are required through extraction on land or the seabed. Such operations will always impact natural habitat and carry a high sustainability risk requiring thorough multidisciplinary assessments. [5]

Biodiversity and renewables. Even though renewables sound good, they are area-intensive and have major implications on the local environment. [6]

Oil/gas and climate. Having deep roots in the Norwegian oil and gas industry, SINTEF is juggling the balancing act of support for safe and efficient oil and gas extraction in existing fields and, at the same time, actively contributing to the transition toward emission-free energy production.[7]

Treasure in a Landfill: Revaluing What We Throw Away

"WHY ARE WE DIGGING FOR NEW gold in Africa when the same can be reclaimed from our old phones?" This thought-provoking question was posed by Erik Solheim in our interview. A distinguished figure, Solheim has served as a UN diplomat, a Norwegian politician, and an activist. He's currently the President of the Belt and Road Green Development Initiative in Beijing and holds positions as a senior adviser at the World Resource Institute and as chief mentor to the Global Alliance for Sustainable Planet.

It's a simple question but sheds light on a growing issue. In today's world, we're too quick to throw our electronic devices away. But what if we started to see them not as junk but as reservoirs of valuable materials?

E-waste, which includes all our discarded electronics such as cell phones, laptops, heaters, toasters, and tablets, are piling up and rapidly becoming one of the most significant waste challenges of the 21st century. With a steady rise in consumer electronics production and consumption, we find ourselves facing mountains of discarded devices. And within these landfills, there is a multitude of hidden critical raw materials and precious metals like gold. In the book, *Wasteland*, it is estimated that up to 7% of the world's gold reserves may currently be contained in E-waste.[8]

Solheim states that studies have shown that there's more gold in a kilo of electronic waste than in a kilo of gold ore in South Africa mines. The mines have been at the forefront of the global gold industry for decades, while the riches in our discarded devices remain overlooked.

Herein lies our challenge: should we continue with the old ways of mining, with its many environmental and human challenges? Or, as Solheim asked me, "Should we start recycling gold from e-waste?"

"Should we start recycling gold from E-Waste?"

Recycling gold from e-waste certainly presents a possible environmentally friendlier alternative to traditional mining. It would also be lucrative. The United Nations University estimates that the value of materials in our e-waste is approximately GPB 5.9 billion annually.[9]

Traditional mining often involves extensive land degradation, water pollution, and the use of harmful chemicals like cyanide, while mining in landfills for old electronics reduces the environmental footprint. However, e-waste also poses health risks to these 'urban miners.' Given the amount of toxic chemicals in landfills, the upcycling of e-waste can lead to respiratory problems and neurological damage, among other health problems, in individuals processing such waste and perhaps those within the area surrounding the processing plant.

Consider my point of view that the best alternative is to change and start upcycling and reusing the materials that are still in our hands. By reusing and upcycling, we're not just saving the environment from the harms of traditional mining or mining landfills, but also valuing materials at a much higher level than before.

From my conversation with Solheim, it is clear we need to change our mindset. Gold and precious materials should not be laid to waste in a landfill. The real task is understanding that our old devices aren't mere waste but treasure troves. The question isn't just about recycling; it's about elevating the worth of what we already have.

How can we change our habits to value the gold and other materials we've so casually thrown away when the devices no longer work?

The raw materials in a car?

When I was at the largest Norwegian business conference, NHO, in 2017, I was reminded about the valuable materials in a car. Erik Osmundsen, the CEO of Norsk Gjenvinning (NG), the leading sustainable waste management services broke down for the audience the raw materials that are in a regular car and demonstrated how 85% of the car is recyclable. That number rises to 95% if you account for the materials that can be converted into fuel to drive other cars.

As Eric correctly states, "We no longer work in the garbage industry but in the recycling of raw materials industry."[10]

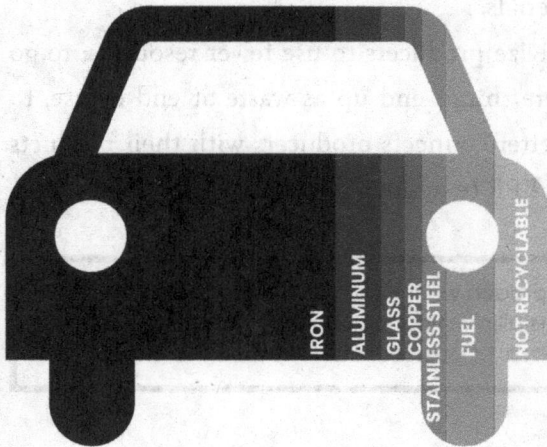

Iron	804 Kilos 1773.32 lbs
Aluminum	64 Kilos 141.10 lbs
Glass	18 Kilos 39.68 lbs
Copper	6 Kilos 13.23 lbs
Stainless Steel	3 Kilos 6.61 lbs
Fuel	104 Kilos 229.28 lbs

*Rough estimate...

Waste management needs the circular economy

Waste management and recycling are often an afterthought and will continue to be until we apply the ideas of a circular economy to the problem. Waste management, reuse, and recycling should be thought of as raw materials that can be reused and designed into any new product.

As I have tried to show with the car example, the materials used to create a car (or really anything) should be designed and built to be repurposed for another future product. As the saying goes: *One man's trash is another man's treasure.*

In her state of the union speech, EU president Ursula von der Leyen addressed some hard facts: "Without secure and sustainable access to the necessary raw materials, our ambition to become the first climate-neutral continent is at risk." [11]

Starting in the design phase, we need to look at how we can go from product maximization to providing human needs, where efficiency is complemented with sufficiency. Additionally, at the product's end-of-life, we should ensure its raw materials are reused, rather than resorting to the extraction of new virgin materials.

Policy makers can incentivize producers to use fewer resources, to go from a linear economy, where things end up as waste at end of use, to a circular economy which better connects producers with their products through the whole chain, *i.e.*, EPR (extended producer responsibility.)

> **EPR** is a policy approach where producers are given a significant responsibility – financial and/or physical – for the treatment or disposal of post-consumer products.

As I see it, policymakers have traditionally had some blind spots that need attention.

Vision and approach. Public leaders lack the capacity and knowledge to translate systemic change into their concrete policies and investment structures, which results in conflicting policies that hinder real transformation.

Demand-side focus. Most policies focus on cleaning up the supply side of our economy, but they often overlook the demand side. This oversight ignores crucial issues like who is responsible and fair distribution and misses out on potential key solutions.

And certainly, resource efficiency vs. energy efficiency. Resource efficiency and energy efficiency might sound alike and are often used interchangeably, but they're not the same. Resource efficiency means using materials and other resources to their fullest – designing for maximum life expectancy, repairability, and recyclability, thus keeping materials at the highest level of value at all times. On the other hand, energy efficiency is about doing the same job or getting the same result but using less energy, like using LED lights instead of old-fashioned bulbs.

These challenges call for innovation and unity. We can shape a future that's sustainable and thriving. Through collaboration, ingenuity, and mindful choices, we can build resilience and an environment for nature and business to thrive.

Navigating Dilemmas Amidst Modern Challenges

EVERY INNOVATION BRINGS its own set of challenges, demanding unique adjustments and adaptations. As we address pressing issues such as environmental sustainability, resource scarcity, and societal well-being, our initial solutions may seem straightforward and well-intentioned. However, as we pursue new solutions, we often find that the path to solving one problem can give rise to a host of new challenges.

Here are examples of these dilemmas that we face:

Batteries rely on extracting lithium, a rare earth material that poses hazards to miners and the environment.

Electric cars, praised for emission reduction, heavily increase the need and use of new materials creating environmental challenges elsewhere

The choice between plastic, paper, and reusable bags involve factors beyond composition, such as production, transportation, energy use, and disposal.

Avocado farming, a staple for vegans, strains the environment due to water scarcity and deforestation.

Excessive scare tactics of environmental warnings can lead to disregard for other legitimate concerns.

Introducing invasive species to control others can worsen ecological imbalances.

Mass production and marketing can turn wants into perceived needs.

These dilemmas occur because the world is intricately interconnected, and our actions can have far-reaching consequences that extend beyond our immediate goals. When we attempt to address complex issues with singular, linear solutions, we may unintentionally overlook or underestimate the various factors and face unintended outcomes that demand further consideration and adjustment.

The pitfalls of linearity in our solutions

Often, we approach problem-solving with a single-minded perspective. We focus solely on a solution, neglecting to consider the holistic or 360-degree view of its potential consequences.

This tunnel vision can lead us astray, causing new challenges to emerge from the very solutions we hoped would resolve issues. As we progress toward a circular economy, our goal is to inspire a broader, longer-term mindset. We want to encourage everyone to step back and look beyond the immediate solution and examine the full spectrum of intended and unintended outcomes. By adopting this comprehensive approach, we can make practical changes that address the problem at hand and pave the way for a more sustainable future. In the next section, we will provide the perfect example of this -- the introduction of the mongoose in Hawaii--where an attempt to control pests ended up causing significant harm to the ecosystem.

The Mongoose of Hawaii: A Tale of Unintended Consequences[12]

During the late nineteenth century, sugar was the dominant crop in Hawaii. However, beneath this façade of agricultural success lurked a problem – rats.

These bothersome rats gnawed through the sugar cane, leaving a trail of destruction. Plantation owners were desperate as their sugar industry was threatened and looked to Jamaica for a solution. In Jamacia, the

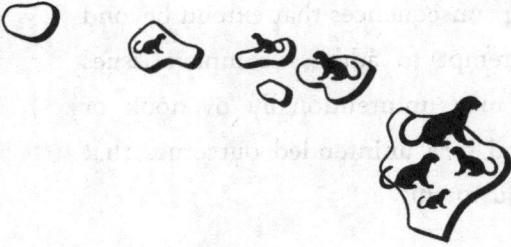

plantation owners had imported the Indian mongoose in 1872 to control the rat population and had been seemingly successful. On paper, it seemed like the perfect solution for Hawaii. A natural enemy to keep the rat populations in check.

Eager for a solution, the plantation owners imported between 1883 and 1900 mongooses that were released into the fields of Hawaii. For a moment, it seemed to be an effective solution.

But nature, in all its complexity, is rarely predictable. Instead of the great mongoose being able to control the rat population, it changed the islands' biodiversity. Birds that had lived without the threat of predators, like the mongoose, found themselves defenseless against this new invader.

The other irony was that the mongoose is the predator of the day, while the rat is the predator of the night. The two rarely crossed paths. Instead of the mongoose controlling the rat population, the mongoose population became the new challenge, a symbol of the unintended consequences of meddling with Mother Nature.

The good news is that nature adapts. Over the years, some species have shown signs of adjusting to the mongoose's presence by altering their behavior, nesting locations, or feeding patterns.

For better or worse, the mongoose has become a part of Hawaii's story. The Hawaiian mongoose project was an imported approach to a local problem. It not only failed to solve the problem but created new ones.

The Hawaiian mongoose is a reminder to be mindful of how easy it is to be linear and focus blindly on finding one solution to a problem; instead, take more time to ask questions– what can be the intended consequences of our solution? By understanding the possible unintended consequences, we can go back to the drawing board and find a more holistic solution. As Alexandra Bech Gjørv stated earlier, we have not found the right solution if there is a dilemma.

Reflection

Do the solutions make sense?

Are they based in science?

Are they good for businesses?

Do they improve the lives of the general public? Or exalt a privileged few?

Will people actually support and carry out the solutions?

How can we inspire people to innovative action?

How do we safeguard against introducing something new to fix a problem that ends up creating a new problem?

IS IT ACTUALLY A SOLUTION? CHECKLIST

- [ ] Does the solution make sense?
- [ ] Is it based in science?
- [ ] Is it good for business?
- [ ] Does it improve the lives of the general public? Or exalt a privileged few?
- [ ] Will people actually support and carry out the solutions?
- [ ] How can we inspire people to innovative action?
- [ ] How do we safeguard against introducing something new to fix a problem that ends up creating a new problem.

Tracing the Origins: How Did We Arrive at a Linear Economy?

SINCE THE ONSET OF COVID-19, I've frequently analyzed the linear economy's roots and the transition to a circular economy. Being confined to our homes and video conferencing via ZOOM or TEAMs as the window to the world offered a silver lining: meeting virtually to discuss various facets of the circular economy with global experts. A common question was: where did it all start? While multiple answers exist, my journey into history revealed some captivating insights.

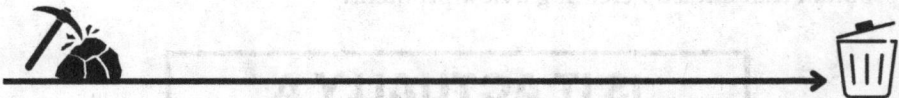

Understanding the nuances of the linear economy requires more than just a dictionary definition. The beginnings of the linear economy didn't suddenly happen with our present-day disposables and single-use items. Before this model dominated, we had different systems, although they weren't without their imperfections. However, it's undeniable that without the linear economy's principles, many of our modern conveniences—cars, electronics, fast fashion—might not have been developed. As we shift back toward a circular society, it's worth noting and giving credit to benefits that we have reaped from the linear model.

Shifting to a circular economy is not the only solution and will not miraculously realize overnight a pristine environment and global prosperity. Yet, I firmly believe that embracing a circular, nature-centric mindset could

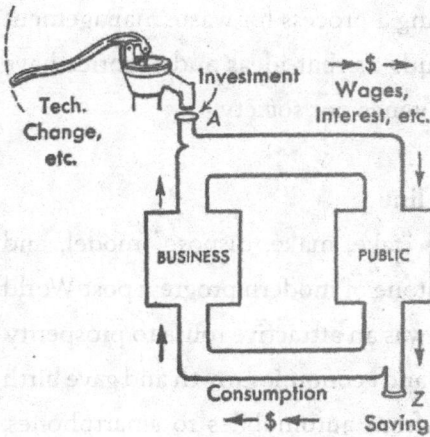

This is the 1948 "Circular Flow Diagram." While this model was successful and used to show the flow of products in a circular way, it is the foundation of the linear economy as it fails to account for waste and access to limited resources.

bring about transformative good. By aligning our economic systems with nature's cyclical processes, we not only nurture our environment but also open doors to more sustainable profitability and innovation within businesses.

In essence, the promise of a cleaner, healthier, and more resilient economy is not a pipe dream—it's a very tangible possibility when we transition toward a circular economy.

The father of modern economics and the linear economy[13]

Paul E. Samuelson was the first American to win the Nobel Memorial Prize in Economic Sciences and is known as the father of modern economics. [14] He popularized simple diagrams like the above *Circular Flow* diagram to explain complex systems to the public.[15] Influenced by economists François Quesnay and Jean-Baptiste Say, he brought the concepts of a linear economy into the education system and popularized economics by communicating in charts and diagrams catered to explaining how our society worked. His picture-rich textbook, "Economics: An Introductory Analysis," first published in 1948, was a critical achievement "and was soon adopted by university professors across the country and overseas." It was a bestselling textbook and is now in the nineteenth edition with nearly four million copies sold in forty languages.[16]

Taking a critical look at Samuelson's *Circular Flow* model reveals that he overlooked waste management. Today, we are confronted with Samuelson's oversight of the importance of designing a process for waste management at the outset. Samuelson's work reminds us that ideas and theories have consequences and can profoundly influence our society.

Linear mindset and Ford's assembly line

The linear economy operates on the "take, make, dispose" model, and Samuelson's diagram became a cornerstone of modern progress post World War II. The rise of the linear economy was an attractive route to prosperity. It ignited technological breakthroughs and economic growth and gave birth to numerous modern conveniences—from automobiles to smartphones. However, the very strengths of the linear model have, over time, revealed themselves as our greatest challenges. The system's focus on short-term windfall and an inherent design and planning process failed to account for product end-of-life. As a result, today we are having to deal with mounting piles of waste, diminishing natural resources, and ecological imbalances.[17]

Samuelson built his theory by codifying the current state of the society in which he was living. In a time ridden with economic insecurities, he was tasked to create an engaging economic study for engineering students at MIT who were ready to rebuild society after World War Two. The linear mindset was already part of society, and Samuelson put words to what people already intuitively knew and lived. I imagine he might have looked back to Ford's famous assembly line concept that had already been in existence since 1913.

Henry Ford revolutionized mass production by popularizing the assembly line to produce his Ford Model T automobile. "The process made it possible to build a Model T in ninety minutes. The price of the car also dropped from $825 in 1908 to $260 in 1925."[18]

"The assembly line revolutionized manufacturing, industry, and society by significantly increasing productivity, reducing costs, and making consumer goods more accessible to a larger population. It has also influenced work culture, urban development, and the global economy."[19]

The new system had a drawback for workers. Instead of teams building a whole car together, workers were required to do the same repetitive and monotonous tasks.

> **DEFINITION:** Assembly line is a way of making products where different parts are put together in a set order. This process divides the work into specific tasks and uses machines and identical parts to make it faster and easier to build the final product.

As I see it the success of the assembly line seeped into all facets of life. To fully understand how we adopted a linear framework, we need to go back to the origins of in United States in the 1920s, a society at the forefront of advancement, which stood almost half a century ahead of the rest of the world.

TAKE   MAKE   DISPOSE

How we got here: mass production and the birth of the modern consumer.

"A change has come over our democracy, it is called 'consumptionism'. The American citizens' first importance to his country is now no longer that of citizen, but that of consumer."

-Samuel Strauss, Journalist and Critic of American Society, "Things are in the Saddle," Atlantic Monthly, November 1924 [20]

Journalist and critic Samuel Strauss articulated the rise of the consumer culture in his writings. His commentary was prominently featured in esteemed publications of the time, including *The Atlantic Monthly* and *The New Republic*.

In the 1920s, the fabric of society was changing rapidly. There are few transformations as profound as the birth of the second wave of mass production. This marvel, which revolutionized the production process, and introduced another seismic transformation: the rise of the mass consumer. In the 20th century, due to the challenges of mass production and the risk of overproduction, people were expertly molded into consumers driven by desires. [21]

After World War I, the challenges of mass production became even more pronounced. Over the next decade, Presidents Harding, Coolidge, and Hoover confronted the issue of businesses making products without enough wealthy consumers to buy them. These leaders preferred a hands-off approach, but they also supported businesses with necessary government help. Their main goal was to boost efficiency and reduce waste, but this effort also reshaped how we viewed the citizen.

Efficiency propels growth

Trained as an engineer and known for his humanitarian efforts, Herbert Hoover recognized the inefficiencies of a lack of industry standards and became a strong advocate for industrial standardization. As Secretary of Commerce under Presidents Harding and Coolidge, he established the Division of Simplified Practice. Through this division, he collaborated with over a hundred different industries, urging them to adopt standardized tools, hardware, building materials, and auto parts. This initiative streamlined production processes, minimized waste in the production process, and enhanced efficiency across industries. [22]

This ripple effect also stimulated growth, and the American industries strengthened their competitive stature globally by delivering high-quality standardized goods at competitive rates. Infrastructure development also received a boost. Standardized building materials resulted in mass expansion of essential structures like roads, bridges, and buildings.

As a result, consumers enjoyed consistent quality and more affordable prices of consumer goods. This shift resulted in the rise of the middle class. However, it also brought an unintended consequence creating a new problem – mass waste of products.

Credit expands the consumer class[23]

The rise of consumer credit, especially in the early 20th century, played a crucial role in shaping the transformation to a consumer society.

While various forms of credit had existed before, the automobile industry, especially through innovative financing like the installment plans from the General Motors Acceptance Corporation (GMAC), revolutionized consumer credit. By offering cars via manageable monthly payments, it not only spurred its own sales but also paved the way for other industries. This innovation made consumer credit a cornerstone of American purchasing habits. For the first time, many products which were previously considered luxuries, became accessible to the average American. Households now flaunted radios, cars, vacuums, and an array of beauty products and fashionable clothing. Through credit, consumers could now purchase these goods and pay later, albeit with added interest and leading to new patterns of consumption.

Advertising & marketing create desire [24]
Addressing a group of advertisers and public relations professionals, President Coolidge astutely observed in 1926 the role that advertising had on mass production:

"Mass production is only possible where there is mass demand. Mass demand has been created almost entirely through the development of advertising." [25]

> "Mass production is only possible where there is mass demand. Mass demand has been created almost entirely through the development of advertising."

I recall, back in the nineties, there was a debate about shopping malls playing subliminal messages behind the cheerful music. Even though I could not hear these messages no matter how hard I tried, experts would claim that my subconscious mind was registering the message, and it was influencing me to take certain actions, like spending more money. Now, I understand why there were protests against the use of background music, and it certainly confirms that advertising can be very advanced and designed to influence people in every psychological and physiological way.

I knew that I was a target, but it was not until I learned about Edward Bernays that I was aware that we all are the targets of constant advertising and information wars that are only getting more and more fierce. While President Coolidge articulated the importance of the consumer, it was Edward Bernays who provided the toolkit to influence them. Drawing from the psychological insights of his uncle, Sigmund Freud, Bernays devised public relations campaigns that delved deep into the psyche of the American public.

Edward Bernays began his influential journey in the realm of public relations during World War I. He played a crucial role in the Committee on Public Information, the U.S. propaganda agency, perfecting techniques to craft and steer public opinion regarding the war efforts.[26]

After World War I, he believed that people's unconscious desires could be tapped into and thereby be able to shape external behaviors — especially in relation to their purchasing decisions. Bernays once remarked, "I decided that if you could use propaganda for war, you could certainly use it for peace. Propaganda got to be a bad word because of the Germans using it. So, I tried to find some other words, which led to 'Counsel on Public Relations.'"[27]

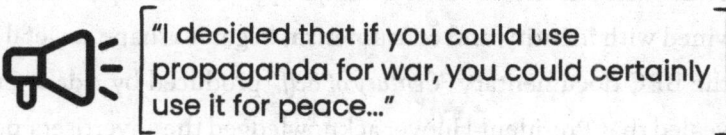

> "I decided that if you could use propaganda for war, you could certainly use it for peace..."

As America advanced into the era of Herbert Hoover, the legacy and influence of Bernays were undeniable. With a foundation in psychology, particularly drawing his inspiration from his uncle Sigmund Freud, Bernays transformed the very nature of public relations. He fervently believed in the power of shaping public opinion and emphasized the importance of creating desires over simply addressing basic needs.

Bernays's revolutionary "Torches of Freedom" campaign in 1929 for the American Tobacco Company reframed the image of a woman smoking in public as an act of rebellion and emancipation. But his influence wasn't just limited to tobacco; he also worked with Proctor & Gamble. For P&G, Bernays transformed the way soap was marketed. Instead of merely presenting it as a cleaning product, he initiated a soap sculpting contest for children, linking the use of the company's soap to creativity and family values. This campaign made soap not just a mundane household item but an essential component of the American family experience, embedding deeper desires within consumers.

By the time of Hoover's presidency, the methodologies pioneered by Bernays were a staple in American advertising, marketing, and public relations. The commercial landscape was being shaped profoundly by such strategies, with businesses and advertisers creating and satisfying the modern consumer culture.

Bernays transformed the narrative from buying based on need to purchasing driven by desire. Through his pioneering campaigns, products were no longer just utilities but symbols of deeper desires and aspirations. For instance, a car wasn't just a mode of transport but a symbol of freedom and status. Such was the power of Bernays' approach that products became intertwined with identity, and consumerism began to shape societal values.

In the BBC documentary *"Century of Self,"* produced by Adam Curtis, it was revealed that President Hoover acknowledged the advertisers' power to reshape society. The shift from fulfilling basic needs to linking desire with necessity marked a significant change. Hoover noted, "You [advertisers] have taken over the job of creating desire and have transformed people into constantly moving happiness machines. Machines which have become the key to economic progress."[28]

1921	1923	1924	1929	1929
Warren G. Harding Becomes President	Calvin Coolidge Becomes President	Strauss calls out consumer culture	Bernay's "Torches of Freedom" Campaign	Herbert Hoover Becomes President

World War I improved America's mass production techniques, but there was an underlying fear that the public couldn't absorb the sheer volume of goods being produced. Hoover's solution was clear – to create an insatiable desire in the public, transforming them from mere citizens to avid consumers.

This sentiment of the era was captured by Paul Mazur of Lehman Brothers (a global financial services company) in 1927: "We must pivot America from a needs to a desires culture. People must be trained to desire, to want new things even before the old had been entirely consumed. We must shape a new mentality in America – man's desires must overshadow his needs."[29]

> The combined visions of Hoover and Bernays, along with the tools of mass production were part of reshaping the 20th century. They transformed passive citizens into active consumers, whose desires and aspirations continue to drive economies and shape societies.

The prosperity of the 1920s ushered in new consumption patterns that ultimately contributed to the 1929 stock market crash. Interestingly, the consumer habits formed during that era continue to persist. The Depression and World War II forced consumers to conserve and reuse items, but they still retained their desires for things they didn't need.

This consumer model provided an engine for economic development and a higher standard of living for many families. However, there were unintended consequences. While Earth's abundant resources enabled the consumer society, there was no incentive to calculate waste or to consider the fact that unlimited production of limited resources was not sustainable over the long run.

For the most part, I see that society has accepted the conclusion that the unlimited production and consumerism model must be replaced with something new. **But we do not know how to stop the consumer engine. We want this transition but are not sure how to move way from a linear system.** I believe the best model for a sustainable future involves natural change starting from the ground up. This model can be best described as the circular economy model.

Can we change our attitudes?

Advertisers, politicians, and thought leaders once collectively steered society toward consumerism, so it stands to reason that a unified effort can direct us toward sustainability. Collaboration between governments, businesses, and consumers can drive meaningful change.

Just as Bernays and others utilized psychology to influence decisions, modern society can use insights from behavioral science to promote sustainable choices.

The rise of consumerism wasn't just an organic phenomenon; it was supported by policies, business models, and economic structures. To move toward a circular economy, systemic changes—ranging from regulations to incentives–are necessary.

Circular economy is the answer for sustainability

The principles of the circular economy are to design out waste, increase product lifespans, and keep resources in use at their highest potential for as long as possible. Instead of the conventional "end-of-life," products are designed for "end-of-use," ensuring they can be reintroduced into the production cycle.

Fortunately, the businesses, government and people around the world are waking up to the fact that the linear economic model is not sustainable and has run its course. I believe that the progress we are seeing is because of the last forty years of academics and theorists providing us with new roadmaps to counter the linear model. Each theory and model has varied nuances to provide us with greater awareness of how to tread forward to ensure that the human footprint is part of a balanced and responsible relationship with our planet, safeguarding its resources for future generations.

How did we get here?

Let's step back and explore how key thinkers have moved away from traditional linear economic models to shape our current understanding and the context of our modern economy.

Beginning in the 1980s, sustainability began to creep into our vocabulary. In 1987, the **United Nations' Brundtland Commission** defined sustainability as "meeting the needs of the present without compromising the ability of future generations to meet their own needs."[30]

By the 1990s, Cradle to Cradle, proposed by Michael Braungart and Bill McDonough, suggested that everything we produce should either return safely to the earth or be completely reusable, prompting us to think long term.

From Janine Benyus, we have **Biomimicry.** This idea draws inspiration from nature to innovate and find solutions, like studying birds to improve plane designs.

There are also groundbreaking approaches like **Industrial Ecology,**[31] **Regenerative Design,** and **Gunter Pauli's Blue Economy**. All these ideas advocate for intelligent resource management and foresight, ensuring we preserve our environment.

Ellen MacArthur's butterfly diagram offers a visual representation of how a circular system can work, showcasing the endless loop of product life cycles and resource usage.

Introduced by **Kate Raworth, Doughnut Economics** reimagines economic models to balance essential human needs and planetary boundaries, ensuring that we thrive within ecological limits. This framework seeks to create a safe and just space for humanity, underlining the importance of not overshooting Earth's environmental ceilings or falling short on life's essentials.

Lastly, the **Conscious Design method** developed by Ian and Jessica Peterman focuses on solutions in the design phase, as 80% of environmental solutions are determined in the design phase. The **Conscious Design method** has four key stages: observation, impact, connection, and inclusion. This approach ensures that designs positively affect society, the environment, and the economy by carefully observing needs, understanding their impacts, connecting within broader systems, and including diverse perspectives.

1980s

Sustainable: The term "sustainable development," defined as "meeting the needs of the present without compromising the ability of future generations to meet their own needs," was coined by the United Nations in their Our Common Future report.

1990s

Cradle to Cradle: Remaking the Way We Make Things published in 1994 by Michael Braungart and Bill McDonough suggests that everything we produce should either return safely to the earth or be completely reusable, prompting us to think long-term.

Biomimicry: Janine Benyus published Biomimicry: Innovation Inspired by Nature. This idea revolves around drawing inspiration from nature to innovate and find solutions, like studying birds to improve plane designs.

Industrial Ecology: The term "industrial ecology" was coined by Robert Frosch and Nicholas Gallopoulos in 1989. It's about making industries work more like ecosystems, where waste from one is used by another, aiming for a zero-waste system. The establishment of the Journal of Industrial Ecology in 1997 further popularized the concept.

2000s

Blue Economy: Gunter Pauli publishes Blue Economy: 10 Years, 100 Innovations, 1000 Jobs, a systems-based approach to the design and development of businesses that takes inspiration from natural systems. It prioritizes sustainability by observing and emulating nature's patterns and strategies to develop efficient and sustainable solutions for societal challenges.

2010s

Butterfly Diagram: Developed by Ellen Macarthur, the Butterfly Diagram offers a visual representation of how a circular system can work, showcasing the endless loop of product life cycles and resource usage.

Doughnut Economy: In 2017 Kate Raworth proposes the "Doughnut Economics" model in her book, Doughnut Economics: Seven Ways to Think Like a 21st-Century Economist. The concept is explained on their website as: "The Doughnut consists of two concentric rings: a social foundation, to ensure that no one is left falling short on life's essentials, and an ecological ceiling, to ensure that humanity does not collectively overshoot the planetary boundaries that protect Earth's life-supporting systems."

2020s

Conscious Design: The Conscious Design concept, coined by Ian Peterman in 2023, is a proactive approach that lays the groundwork for creating products that are inherently circular, asserting that 80% of environmental solutions are determined in the design phase. By anticipating problems before they arise, this method focuses on designing sustainable solutions upfront rather than retroactively addressing the consequences. Grounded in observation, impact, connection, and inclusion, it ensures that every design positively influences social, environmental, and financial spheres, fosters alignment within ecosystems and communities, and champions diversity and equity in the design and educational sectors.

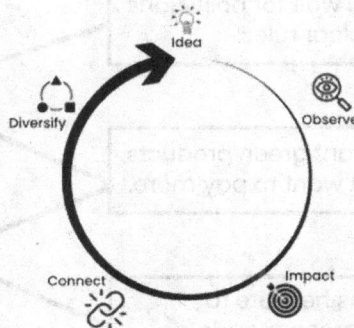

Trapped in a System

"How many people are trapped in their everyday habits:
part numb, part frightened, part indifferent? To have a
better life we must keep choosing how we are living."
- ALBERT EINSTEIN

I HAD THE OPPORTUNITY to interview Per Espen Stoknes, who is not only an economist and psychologist but also an author and professor at BI Norwegian Business School. Our discussion took us into the complexities of breaking a system on which everyone relies. To paraphrase Stoknes, we are confronted with a paradox –

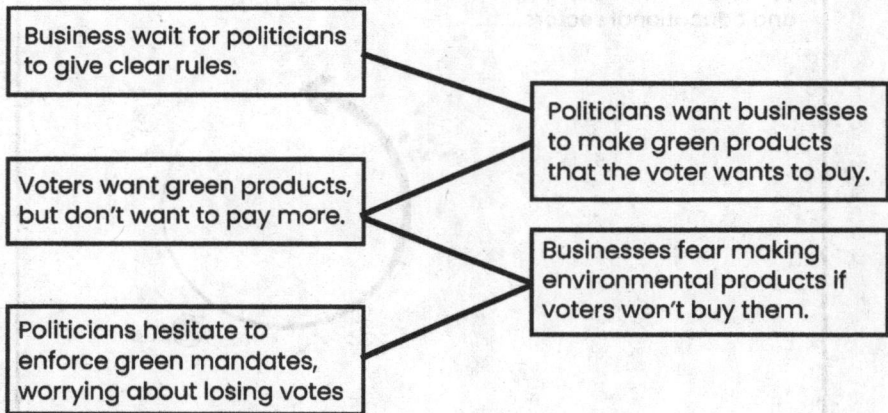

Business wait for politicians to give clear rules.

Politicians want businesses to make green products that the voter wants to buy.

Voters want green products, but don't want to pay more.

Businesses fear making environmental products if voters won't buy them.

Politicians hesitate to enforce green mandates, worrying about losing votes

Bjørn K Haugland is the CEO of SKIFT, a Norwegian business-led climate initiative aiming to accelerate the transition to a low-carbon economy. Bjørn explains the journey and waste produced by a simple paper cup.

"Think about the journey of a paper cup. It is produced in China, then it travels from deep within western China, using diesel, to the port. From there, it gets transported to Europe, gets shuffled on a smaller ship, and finally it arrives at this event organized by some entity. Then someone drinks from the paper cup, and afterward, it disappears into another value chain. It is one of the many bizarre examples of how we use and overconsume resources."

This story is a concrete example of the linear system and causes many to think *this just the way things are.*

Bjørn added,

> "The day you put your foot down or genuinely live up to what you say you'll do, things happen. And I believe that we, as business leaders, must have the ability and desire to invest and dare to make mistakes."

Stuck in a mountain of trash

My work in the waste and recycling industry over the last two decades requires me to travel the world. I have seen how other countries handle the trash they collect and get stuck in the process of managing the trash. Trash collection is a colossal burden and a very significant focus of public policy. "Today, the solid waste industry contributes to 5% of all global greenhouse gas emissions – more than the entire shipping and aviation industries combined."[32] I think we want to re-invent how trash is stored, but basically trash handling is the same today as twenty to forty years ago. There is just so much you can do with trash. Yes, modern landfills are better than old ones, but they are still landfills. European landfills are declining, but those in other wealthy countries are not. The US sends fifty percent of waste to landfills, while Australia sends thirty percent. [33] Currently, thirty-seven percent of waste worldwide is landfilled. Another third ends up on open dumpsites that lack environmental controls as required by the more "sanitary" landfills. [34]

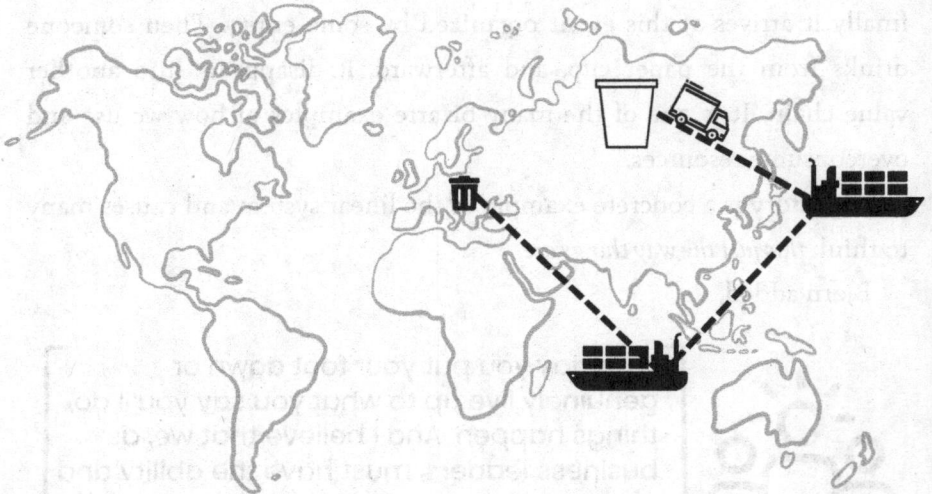

But are landfills sanitary? A landfill is more regulated and might be better than dumps that are not regulated, but to see a landfill mountain of trash is indescribable. I remember when I was in Germany and for the first time saw not just one, but several mountains of trash built upon collected and compiled waste. As Germans are stereotypically viewed as punctual, efficient, and disciplined, the trash mountains I saw were horrifically impressive in both their scale and how the trash had been sorted. There was a method and a reason as to why it was gathered like it was.

I thought that if we only took the kind of meticulous care to find a solution to sustainability as we do for sorting trash, then we would have a chance to truly make an impact. It also made me realize the overwhelming level of consumption that exists and made me more self-conscious about my own materialistic use.

These landfills in Germany are carefully engineered and managed in a manner where waste is isolated from the environment and designed to minimize environmental risks. They use protective liners to prevent groundwater contamination and systems to collect and treat leachate and methane gas. I believe landfills should not be the answer, as they pose a great threat to the environment, with the possibility of leaks contaminating ground water and land. There are many sanitary landfills, managed by organizations like Suez Waste Management, that guarantee secure storage of waste around the world. Something in my gut, however, says no to this kind of solution.

When we went to Mexico City, our experience was different. As to be expected in any densely populated area, trash had accumulated—but instead of being collected, sorted, and placed in mountains like it was in Germany, it was everywhere. In the gutters, on the streets, and in small ravines that had become dump sites for everything. You could say we had already become accustomed to clean beaches, so to speak, and for us experience the opposite was heartbreaking.

In low-income countries, ninety-three percent of waste ends up dumped while in high-income countries the figure is only two percent. Dumps are open areas where waste is simply thrown without any measures to manage it. As a result, dumps pose even greater risks to the environment and public health, often leading to water contamination, air pollution, and other hazards.

And we waste so much – worldwide in 2016, the last year with reliable figures, we produced 2.1 billion metric tons of solid waste.[35] The richer we are, the more we consume and the more we waste. Consider that one third of what we throw away today consists of things produced the same year.

"A third of the food we produce worldwide is wasted, and yet 820 million people go hungry every day "

The worst thing is that we have created a system where food is expected to look a certain way, resulting in farmers losing up to 40 of their crops due to not meeting supermarket standards.

At RENAS, we specialize in managing the collection and safe disposal of WEEE, an acronym for Waste Electrical and Electronic Equipment. This category includes anything using electricity, including items ranging from old computers and refrigerators to TVs. Alarmingly, this is the fastest-growing waste in the world. What makes the concern even more significant is that only 17.4 percent of electronics are recycled. As previously discussed, there's a literal 'gold mine' in landfills due to the precious and rare materials contained within electronics. On average, a single electronic device can hold as many as 60 different elements. For instance, a typical iPhone contains 0.018 grams of gold,[36] 0.34 grams of silver, 0.015 grams of palladium,[37] and a minuscule amount of platinum. These quantities may seem insignificant, but in terms of density, you'd find ten to fifty times more copper in a metric ton of electronics than in a metric ton of copper ore.[38]

While we can get discouraged by the current situation, understanding where we stand can guide us toward a clearer vision for the future we want. By visualizing a brighter future, the existing problems will become more evident and not as easy to brush under the carpet. When we can visualize or even just imagine a better situation, we change the status quo from waste being an overlooked issue to one that needs attention and action.

A circular system works with nature, not against it
Breaking out of a system is hard.

Have your ever been pressured to be or do something you are not?

I have two older brothers, who were often tasked with watching over me. I would follow them around and get involved in activities that I like to think I would not normally do if it were not for their influence. One time, my brother wanted to make some extra money by collecting recyclable bottles. In Norway, by collecting four bottles and turning them in, you could afford a Snickers bar. This seems innocent enough, but not the way my brothers went about it. My brothers and I would go to the brewery to get bottles, then trade them at the store. As the youngest and shortest, they would have me stand guard by the entrance, while they snuck into the brewery to "collect" bottles to recycle.

As a young child, I did not fully comprehend the gravity of what we were doing, yet even as young as I was, I knew deep inside that it was going against the values I had been taught by my parents. But for me at the time it was more important to have the approval of my brothers. The allure of feeling included with my cool brothers were stronger incentives than telling it to my parents. I found myself feeling trapped in this activity.

After a couple of times, I became more aware of the seriousness of what we were doing and the negative impact it could have on others. I eventually found the courage to stop.

The first time you stand up for what you believe, and you go against the grain, it's scary. I knew that I might get picked on for not participating and would potentially not be included in other activities, and yet, it was a liberating experience. It taught me that there is always a way out of a difficult situation, even if it may not be immediately apparent.

As we get older, we put our foot down more and at times we choose not to. It's a process to work ourselves up to say no to the pressure, but when we do, it is liberating. Saying no can align our priorities and our decisions with our inner values.

We can feel trapped in small groups, like I was with my brothers, but at this local level we have autonomy to say no. The harder part is when we feel trapped in a greater group or system and feel we do not matter.

The Sheep

WE SAY THAT SHEEP ARE DUMB, because they will follow the sheep in front of them regardless of where it goes and not ask questions. The next sheep will do the same, and so on, and so on. If the leading sheep is literally running off a cliff, with disastrous consequences, the others will follow it to their deaths. What would happen if just one sheep stopped and brought to the attention of the others that this path was no good? One can only assume that when people are acting like sheep, it provides an excellent opportunity for a leader to step up with a new plan.

Sheep aren't really dumb. They are flock animals and will instinctively move in groups. Mostly this serves them well, but sometimes they fall prey to their flock mentality.

Like sheep, we are social beings. Just as sheep follow the lead of one member of the flock, we humans often find ourselves influenced by the actions and decisions of those around us. This phenomenon is not unlike the herd instinct observed in sheep, where the safety and cohesion of the group are prioritized.

[The majority of people are willing to follow, but are simply waiting for a leader to step forward and show a better way.

At first, it doesn't really matter what or who this is, or how it comes about, just as long as there is something or someone leading us. I have personally found myself stuck in traffic when one driver takes action trying to resolve their situation and leads a flow of other drivers do the same thing. Even if my first reaction is that this is not a good solution, I have still found myself following like a sheep, only to end up in a worse-off situation than before. Isn't it amazing how we turn the blame around to someone else at the first opportunity?

It's easy to become trapped in a system without even realizing it. Systems are all around us, from the education system to the political system to the economic system. We are born into them, and they shape our lives in ways we may not fully comprehend.

Sometimes, these systems can limit our choices, constrain our actions, and even prevent us from realizing our full potential. We may feel like we are stuck in a cycle that we cannot break out of, or that the system is too big and powerful for us to challenge. We may also be influenced by social norms, cultural values, and other factors that reinforce the system's status quo. It's important to recognize that systems are not natural or inevitable but are created and sustained by human actions and decisions. Only by acknowledging the existence of the system and actively working to change it can we hope to break free from its hold and create a better future for ourselves and others. Knowing that others are waiting for leaders to follow, I invite you to find your own way to publicly promote a more circular lifestyle as part of your green path. Why not multiply your own effort and impact?

The impact of the black sheep

As we explored previously, people tend to follow, and often give themselves a free pass when they see others leading, even if it means being led down an unhelpful or unhealthy path. "Well, that other person did it, so it must be okay" is often the mentality.

Not far from where I grew up, there was a swimming place that we would frequent. It had a trash can, and most of the time people were conscious of cleaning up after themselves. We all wanted to leave the place nice for the next people coming to enjoy nature and a nice swim, right? Once in a while, though, we would observe someone behaving differently. If someone missed the trash can, it usually didn't take long for others to miss it too, or simply not bother to clean up at all. ("Well, they didn't, so why should we?") The magnetism of that initial negative action, and how contagious it is, makes for a scary observation.

Who hasn't been in a park after an event, looking at all the trash on the ground? And even though it is a shock, we still do not start to clean it up. You can even argue it is cultural. Next time you travel, spend some time observing. What do you see? Do the streets have trash cans for people to sort the trash more easily? Are the freeways littered with garbage along the roadside?

From sheep to Leadersheep [39]

During my research for this book, I made a fascinating discovery: a special breed of sheep in Iceland called the Leadersheep. These sheep are different from the usual flock mentality we associate with their kind. With just 1,400 in the world, [40] Leadersheep are known for their independence, intelligence, and courage. They take charge within their herds, guiding the group's pace and well-being.

Interestingly, scientists believe Iceland's challenging weather conditions might be the reason for this unique trait. It's almost as if these sheep needed leaders to navigate through tough times. Drawing a parallel between the Leadersheep and humans, we find an intriguing reflection of our own nature. The Leadersheep's ability to adapt and lead in challenging circumstances underscores the importance of having individuals who can navigate uncertainty. In a world embracing the circular economy, such leaders are crucial.

Unlike sheep, humans possess a higher level of consciousness and reasoning. We can make intentional choices based on our values, beliefs, and knowledge. While the herd instinct may still influence us, our ability to critically assess information sets us apart. Just as the Leadersheep strike a balance between following the flock and asserting leadership, humans can blend collective action with individuality. In the circular economy, we need individuals who can guide us toward sustainable practices and innovation, much like the Leadersheep guiding their herd through adverse conditions.

"You Matter More Than You Think"

You might feel stuck in the *system*, but the path to changing that system is easier than it may seem.

In a conversation with Karen O'Brien, a professor at University of Oslo and the author of "You Matter More Than You Think," we delved into the human connection and practical strategies for breaking free from this system. While discussing theories of change is a starting point, true transformation emerges from taking action. Our conversation revealed how swiftly businesses are willing to adapt once the trailblazers have demonstrated the viability of new solutions.

How do we find the courage to make uncomfortable choices as individuals? The answer lies in reflecting on the impact of environmental change on our human experience—our sense of security, vulnerability, and adaptability. Are we trapped in a cycle of self-sabotage that's hard to break?

These questions are tough but crucial. While we might not have immediate answers, we do have enough knowledge to make small changes. Karen's understanding of human psychology reveals that people often fear the uncertainty of change. Yet, once committed, they realize how little effort it takes to create change, whether on an individual or collective level.

As Karen articulates,

> "It's so easy to say, 'You must change' instead of thinking of us as change agents who can transform ourselves and others."

While the idea of being "change agents" is attractive, the actual changes we make, like switching from flights to trains, could make vacations longer and more costly. Even switching to electric cars might only bring a small reduction in the larger context of oil consumption.

Karen recognizes the challenge of reconciling personal change with societal systems. However, our awareness can empower us to effect change from within.

Her message resonates. Though we may feel insignificant, making climate-conscious choices in our daily lives carries more impact than we realize.

Last year, she penned "You Matter More than You Think," emphasizing that when we reduce ourselves to mere individualists, we underestimate the potential for change. Rather than merely aspiring to "be the change you want to see," we must actively embody and lead that change.

At the heart of this issue lies our relationship with ourselves, our environment, and the future. Acknowledging and confronting the complex emotions tied to change allows us to reassess our connection to the world around us. This prompts us to take an active role in shaping the future and to be more mindful of nurturing our planet.

Adopting essential environmental changes can feel overwhelming, especially for those who don't follow rules to the letter. But we don't need strict mandates to make a difference. We can all have an impact by embracing common values and purposefully taking action in our daily lives.

Wherever we live, just about everyone shares common values and a desire to leave a sustainable legacy. Achieving this entails reshaping the narrative and redefining our relationship with materials, which directly influences our rapport with the climate. Ultimately, the quality of our presence and the value we contribute to society matter more than blind adherence to rules.

Effectively understanding and addressing environmental change requires a multifaceted approach encompassing personal, political, and practical dimensions of transformation. These realms provide theoretical frameworks for comprehending how environmental shifts affect individuals and societies, as well as how we can aptly respond to these changes.

To foster effective responses to environmental change, we must overhaul personal attitudes, engage in political action to catalyze institutional change, and implement practical solutions to tackle emerging challenges. By addressing these three dimensions of transformation, we can forge a sustainable and resilient future for ourselves and generations to come.

We just need a few to change the system

Karen O'Brien emphasizes that change doesn't require convincing everyone. A smaller group can ignite a change. Historical shifts rarely demanded a majority. Tipping points show that when some people choose alternatives like electric cars or quitting smoking, it influences others. Could this principle work for personal climate actions too?

A journey from peace to climate: Karen O'Brien's *green pivot*

Karen O'Brien's transformative journey dates back to the scorching summer of 1988, a pivotal moment when she was introduced to the concept of global warming. From her varied experiences growing up—spanning from the bustling streets of Bangkok to the serene beaches of Westport, Connecticut—O'Brien's diverse background set the stage for her future pursuits.

While initially inclined toward a diplomatic career, O'Brien's path took a sharp turn after she encountered an unprecedented heatwave that captured the world's attention. Intrigued by this event, she embarked on a scientific exploration, eventually finding her way into the realm of climate research with a focus on its human aspects. Today, as a climate professor at the University of Oslo and a contributor to both the UN's climate and nature panels, O'Brien embodies her personal *green pivot* that began in 1988. Her ongoing efforts reflect her dedication to doing her part in shaping a more sustainable future.

Takeaways from being trapped in linear system

Human actions and decisions shape systems, influencing our choices and potential. Identifying these systems and actively working to change them can pave the way for a brighter future.

Small steps matter—simple changes in our routines can have a significant positive impact on ourselves and others. Gradually integrating more adjustments into our daily lives creates lasting change.

Fear might hold us back, but it can also fuel our drive to excel. Embracing uncertainty can lead to increased productivity and successful outcomes.

While achieving 100 percent participation may not be necessary, collective effort drives societal change. And interestingly, research suggests that a committed minority might be enough to initiate a tipping point that triggers widespread change.

To create a more sustainable future, we must adjust our thinking beyond traditional linear models and adopt a more comprehensive approach that promotes sustainable practices. This requires a fundamental change in our mindset and the way we do business. It necessitates collaboration to create closed-loop systems where waste is reduced to a minimum and resources are reused and recycled to create new value.

The Lorax, A Cautionary Tale

> "Business is business!
> And business must grow
> regardless of crummies in tummies, you know.
> I meant no harm. I most truly did not.
> But I had to grow bigger. So bigger I got.
> I biggered my factory. I biggered my roads.
> I biggered my wagons. I biggered the loads...I went
> right on biggering...
> And I biggered my money, which everyone needs."

—Lorax, The Lorax, Dr. Seuss

DR. SEUSS'S *The Lorax* is a cautionary tale that underscores the fragility of our planet. It tells the story of the Lorax, a creature defending the trees against the Once-ler's insatiable desire for them. The area of Thneedville deteriorates due to Once-ler's unyielding desire to acquire more trees and grow bigger and better industries. As the consequences of such greed become clear, the Lorax intervenes, championing balance and respect for nature. Although the tale starts in a bleak setting, it ends with a beacon of hope, suggesting it's never too late for positive change.

The story is a reminder that when we alter one aspect of our environment, it can have far-reaching and unexpected consequences.

While *The Lorax* can be a sobering read in some parts, the title character ultimately brings awareness and education to the people of Thneedville, and they work together to repair the damage that's been done. The underlying message is clear: we need to have reverence for our environment and all the living creatures that call it home. By respecting our planet, we can preserve it for ourselves and for future generations. Another message of the Lorax is that mindsets can change and when they do, transformation is possible.

Society has, for the most part, recognized that we can't continue consuming resources at our current rate and expect everything to be fine for future generations. A change is imperative, and we all have a role to play in making it happen. The first step is for each of us to recognize that change begins with ourselves.

Increasingly, ordinary people, even those who don't consider themselves environmentalists, are beginning to reflect on their own consumption habits and to make conscious choices that prioritize sustainability. There are more people interested in reducing their reliance on single-use plastics, choosing energy-efficient appliances, willingly recycling, and generally supporting companies that prioritize environmental stewardship.

Where does society fit into the Lorax story? There are still plenty of Lorax's out there, but they are fewer than even a decade ago. From my perspective, society has reached the recognition phase, has taken major strides in changing its mindset, and is in the first stages of repairing the damage.

Dr. Seuss provided a wonderful service to mankind by offering the Lorax story to younger generations, who are still developing their mindsets about the world in which they live. This story warns of the dangers of unrestrained growth and forces us to think about the consequences of our actions. However, despite the depiction of bleak devastation, we are left hopeful as the story suggests that positive change is possible and individual actions are powerful.

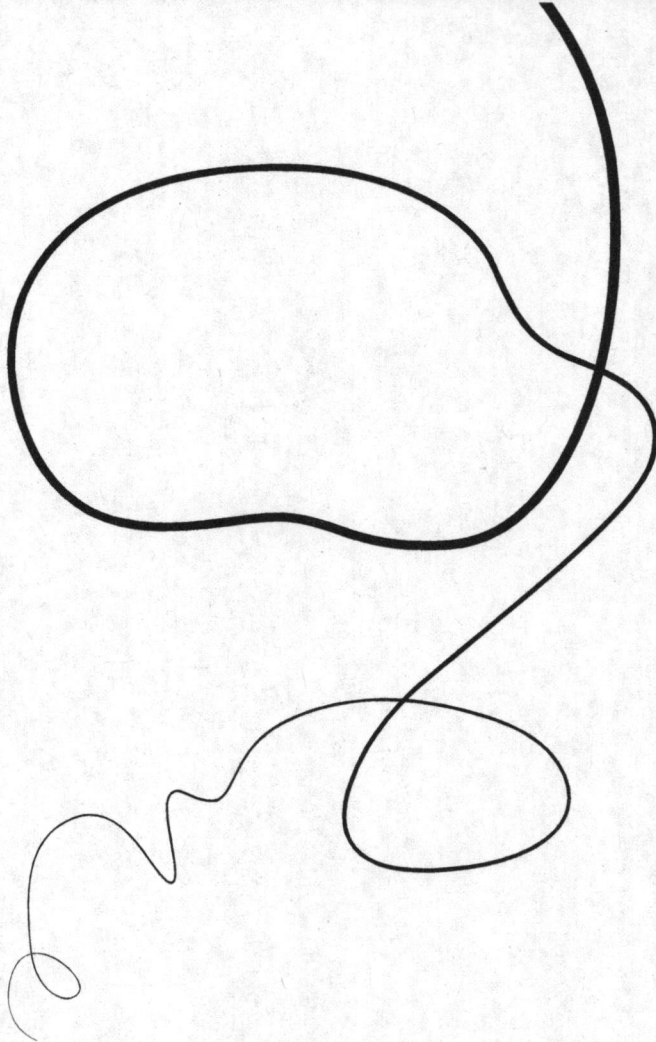

chapter two

the barrier to change...
is change

In this chapter, we're tackling a key issue:

change is hard because it's, well, change.

We will explore the barriers that make change challenging. Despite being necessary, change is often difficult to achieve as it brings discomfort and uncertainties. We will examine a real-life dilemma with oil exploration and the industry's efforts to balance economic interests with environmental responsibility. This chapter aims to provide an insightful, comprehensive view of the complex nature of change and how small changes, in the long run, might be the best change.

Change

Change

Change

Who wants change?

Who wants to change?

CHANGE IS INEVITABLE. Change is hard, and I would argue we are mostly unaware of our limits and barriers. And even when we're aware of them, I would argue that many of us unconsciously choose not to challenge our limits and barriers, because it makes our lives easier in the short run. We don't want to change.

It is easier to continue with my habits and daily routines, going along with the norms of my culture, society, or whatever. If I just close my eyes for a while, it will probably pass, and I won't have to get involved. There's just so much else I have to do and deal with.

This may be an understandable reaction, but if you feel uneasy about something in your life, shouldn't you at least address it within your own mind, take some sort of stand, instead of just continuing along the same path and seeing what happens?

How will the change benefit society and culture?

? • Yet another question arises: are the problems actually problems?
• Or are they symptoms pointing to a deeper cause?
• So, are the solutions even necessary?
• Is there a way around all of this?
• Is there a way to make things simple and practical?
• Maybe there are some basic principles that can be adopted that will yield greater results?

These are questions I want to discover answers to and want to ignite more people to join me in creating a world with sensible solutions to problems.

I admit, not everything can be simple. The very subject of the environment is complex and multifaceted, so how can we truly be practical? Well, I believe it's possible. I believe we improve the lives of billions of people and preserve nature by adopting a more circular economy, a nature-based mindset that lifts all of humanity and inspires to keep going.

Why change?

First, we must establish the reason for change. Why should we change? Individuals, businesses, and governments need to be inspired or provoked to want to change.

Any change starts with a problem, something that is holding you back from progressing forward. A recent example could be COVID, which radically altered our way of living. One notable change is that we now lead lives adjusted to video conferences and haven't gone back. Most events now offer the option of video attendance or in-person participation. While this change was prompted by an uncomfortable situation, the unintended consequences are that people are reducing the amount of driving they have to do and thus reducing their impact on nature. When businesses started seeing that working from home actually worked and that it contributed to cleaner air, they started embracing it more. I like to call this a *green pivot*.

Can you recall when something changed in your life, and you made the decision not to return to the way it used to be? When you opted for conscious choices, like buying secondhand or waiting to trade in your phone?

A circular economy in itself may be a *green pivot* for some. When people get inspired by others' actions, it's contagious and starts a ripple effect. When people see problems being solved and incentivized and not perpetuated or shrouded in fear, they may be compelled to push themselves further toward innovating more sustainable practices in their lives and businesses.

So why change? Because change is human, change can mean a better life for ourselves and our loved ones. If we do not change, what will happen? Will nature change? Will we continue to lose biodiversity, degrade our health, and exhaust resources? These things are already changing. And if we don't change now, we will be forced to change in the future if the resources we depend on are no longer available.

Facts and scare tactics rarely cause change

In 2006, *An Inconvenient Truth* opened in cinemas in the United States. The documentary about the threats to our climate made an indelible mark and certainly raised public awareness, but did it translate into action? There have been studies that showed that tangible behavior change did occur, but it was not always long-lasting.

While the documentary was incredibly powerful, it wasn't necessarily empowering. Polarized positions on climate science continue among party leaders, influencing public polarization on climate change to this day.[41]

Some environmental problems have become critical and that can trigger our innate fight-or-flight response. It's a powerful motivation for quick action, and that point is not lost on activist groups. Scare tactics can be very effective in the short term, but when any alarm is overused or abused, people eventually stop responding to it. Just ask *the boy who cried wolf*. Wolves, like threats to the environment, are very real, but overusing an alarm can turn it into background noise. Fear is powerful but fleeting. It is not an emotion that can be sustained for long.

We have already discussed how scare tactics can make the problem seem too big to manage. Too much alarmism can actually dampen motivation. Action is based on faith that our actions will have consequences. If individuals and companies seem to be less responsive to scare tactics about the environment, it may be that the messaging is becoming obsolete. Could it be that the people are progressing beyond the primitive mindset, and it's the messaging that needs to be abandoned?

Conquering Fear

"Fear is reaction courage is decision."

-Winston Churchill

YEARS AGO, I was rock climbing with a friend of mine. I consider myself an experienced climber, but the route my friend had picked for us was just above my comfort level. I had faith, though, in my friend (who was a more skilled climber than I was), so I trusted the process and followed him. Still, to this day, I consider this route the hardest I've ever climbed.

Nearing the top of the mountain, we were on a wall, anchored in. It was 200 meters (about 650 feet) to the bottom, and we were inching our way up the final stretch. While on this wall, my friend, ahead of me and setting the anchors, turned to me and started yelling at me not to fall. Finding it weird, but funny in a strange way, I laughed at him, replying that of course, I wouldn't fall! He kept repeating it several times over, and I kept assuring him that I was in a good spot, had a good grip, and was in no danger of falling.

It was then he informed me that he was unable to secure the anchor point the way he wanted; it was fastened less than an inch into the small crevasse. Both of us were athletic and not light, so what he was telling me was that the anchor point was able to hold him, but not both of us.

As I looked down at the distance to the bottom, adrenaline started rushing through me, and fear set in. Knowing the immediate danger any misstep or miscalculation would have, I had to mentally reset. I took a few seconds, then continued, and we made it to the top.

What I learned about myself that day was that fear is only in your mind, and that I had to focus all my mental and physical strength to not fail. My current position on the mountain didn't allow me to sit down and contemplate my actions that had led me to this situation, or to go over the risks and the dangers. I had to act, and I had to act in the moment. So, I allowed myself a few seconds of pep talk, talking myself out of the fear and back into success.

Everyone, in any situation, needs to realize that fear is not dangerous in itself. In fact, fear can be a helper. We can train our brains to control our way of thinking to trust ourselves and our actions in the face of it.

Training your brain to let go of fear is a mental exercise, and it is something everyone can do. Every day we will encounter scenarios where our brains will react and fall back on the primitive responses that have been embedded there since we were in caves.

Of course, we are not facing the same dangers today. There are no saber-toothed tigers hunting us, but there are other dangers, minor or big, that will stimulate the same response.

We are all wired differently. While some of us get scared easily, there are others that feed on fear and seek it. I don't want you to seek out dangerous situations, far from it. But you need to be prepared, and you need to learn the skills to overcome fear and conquer it.

When we learn to rewire our brains, we are in better control of our own reactions to our surroundings and can give ourselves small pep talks when needed. And when we are able to do this, we are in a better situation to *act* when we need to act.

Complexity can hinder change[42]

A significant barrier preventing many from making their *green pivot*, may simply be due to overly complex messaging. If we make the problem too big or too complex, attention falls, and the path forward gets blurry. No action is ever taken, because nobody is on the same page of what actually will bring a marked change.

When trying to garner support for policies around protecting the environment, policymakers should focus on keeping it simple and straightforward. People will get turned off, and you will most likely lose necessary support as the complexity rises. There is also a potential for the initiative to be viewed as disingenuous and even perhaps sneaky if it is practically impossible to understand without having a law degree.

Grabbing the attention of your constituents is not always easy, and it's even more difficult to generate action toward some goal. Taking a cue from Donald Miller's book, "Building a StoryBrand," can help to create a narrative and messaging framework that will engage and activate your people. Supporters should be able to explain exactly how your proposed policy will improve their life and what steps they need to take.[43]

Additionally, addressing Maslow's hierarchy of needs will propel an initiative to the next level and help overcome barriers to change that constituents may have. When each subsequent need is fully realized, it's easier to take action. Focusing on *realizing your potential* will help inspire people to change. People's basic needs need to be met before they will take the time to restructure their lives toward something new.

Mike McHargue, a scientist and podcaster mentioned in the book "Building a StoryBrand" by Donald Miller, spent fifteen years assisting tech companies in understanding their customers' thinking. His main finding is that the biggest significant challenge in marketing and communication is excessive complexity. Our brains struggle to process overly complicated information. To make it more digestible, it's better to present information in a storytelling format.

As explained in "Building a StoryBrand," Mike emphasized that the primary function of the brain can be understood via Maslow's hierarchy of needs. First, the brain focuses on ensuring physical survival through eating and drinking, followed by securing a job and dependable income. Second, the brain concerns itself with safety, having a roof over one's head, and a sense of well-being and power to avoid vulnerability. After addressing these basics, the brain focuses on connection and developing relationships with their inner circle of loved ones. It then seeks respect recognition from others. Finally, it deals with self-actualization, the achievement of its full potential.

Mike's insights, as outlined in Donald Miller's book, align with the author's emphasis on the human tendency to constantly seek information that aids their survival instincts. When complex issues like the *circular economy* are presented, people often tune out because their primitive survival instincts are not engaged.

As Donald Miller points out, "All great stories are about survival – physical, emotional, relational, or spiritual."

Our psychology is deeply rooted in our evolutionary past. As early humans, we relied heavily on, the part of the brain that controls primitive reactions such as the fight-or-flight response. Although we no longer face the same imminent life-threatening situations as our ancestors, our brains have preserved the same fundamental structure and tendencies. As a result, past endeavors to influence environmental policy may have heavily relied on tapping into our primal fight-or-flight responses, playing on fear and anxiety. This can sometimes result in us making instinctive choices that are not necessarily the best decisions in the long run. For example, we may

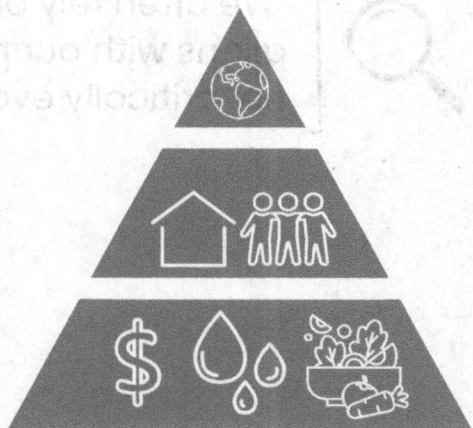

choose to consume more than we need or use environmentally harmful products, because they provide us with immediate gratification or status or immediate relief from a perceived immediate threat.

Recognizing and understanding these underlying psychological tendencies can help us make more informed and conscious decisions about our consumption and lifestyle choices. It is important to consider not just the short-term benefits but also the long-term consequences and impact on the environment and future generations.

Confirmation bias often hinders change

We tend to favor information that agrees with our current beliefs and ignore what contradicts them. According to authors Mercier and Sperber in their book "The Enigma of Reason," our ability to cooperate sets us apart.[44] They argue that our thinking didn't evolve primarily to solve complex problems or analyze new data but to help us navigate life in groups. Reason, in their view, isn't about supporting our beliefs; it's about collaborating with those we trust in our social groups, which was essential for survival throughout our evolutionary history. This means we often rely on information that aligns with our peer groups and may not critically evaluate it.

> We often rely on information that aligns with our peer groups and may not critically evaluate it.

Doing Things the Way They Have Always Been Done 45

FOR A LONG TIME, burning waste was considered a responsible and environmentally friendly solution for disposing of our trash. Subsequently, it became evident that incinerating waste is detrimental to the environment, as it emits harmful toxins into the atmosphere. These pollutants, present in the air, pose a risk when breathed in by people and animals, and they also settle on the ground, affecting water bodies, soil, and vegetation.

These findings were presented in Norway's first Circularity Gap Report – an in-depth analysis of how Norway consumes raw materials to fuel social needs. RENAS sponsored the report with circular frontrunner organizations in Norway, such as Elektroforeningen, Virke, and SKIFT and others. The report stated that Norway has one of the world's highest consumption rates per capita and unveiled that the Norwegian circularity rate is only 2.4 percent. The report delivers a roadmap for increasing circularity and cutting emissions by restructuring business and industry through actions in six key sectors of Norway. It also highlights questions such as:

How good are we at material efficiency?

How much of our materials are circling back into the supply chain and the economy?

One interesting recognition is that when the Norwegian Gap report stated that burning waste created more harm than good and new solutions needed to be created, the industry experienced significant harassment from other industries.

The Norwegian Circularity Gap report is part of The Circularity Gap reporting initiative by the Dutch organization Circle Economy

Foundation. In 2018, they launched the first Circularity Gap Report at the World Economic Forum in Davos to establish a global baseline for circularity, monitor its development, and deliver key actions bridging the circularity gap.

The world was only 9.1 percent circular. In 2023, it was 7.2 percent, meaning more than ninety percent of the materials are never circled back into the economy.

Being 100 percent circular is not possible, or realistic. Of the 92.8 billion tons of material used in 2018, about 36 billion tons was put into stock, meaning long-lasting structures such as roads and buildings.

Still, over fifty-five percent (51.9 billion tons) remained unaccounted, dispersed into the environment as emissions or unrecoverable wastes. The numbers were disheartening. The circularity gap was massive and obviously not sustainable over time.

Taking a step back, we realized a lot of resentment and reluctance to change was linked to history, prestige, and, of course, money tied into well-established routines.

Doing things the way they have always been done is dangerous. It prevents us from taking necessary and innovative action. Today we welcome a shift in this attitude. It is refreshing to know that the circular economy is becoming more accepted. At the same time, there are still old connections toward linear waste flow. It was only after the Circularity Gap Report was presented that it dawned on the industry that we need a more wholesome approach to the circular economy. There is a lack of education on the subject, so the mindset around the concept is still growing. But by being open to new ideas and approaching change with careful consideration, we can transform from "We've always done it this way" to "What are we going to do better?"

| We've always done it this way | (>) | What are we going to do better? |

Freedom of thought and expression are oxygen to a circular economy

What happens when information is controlled and free thought and expression are suppressed? For those with control over the platforms that provide social discourse, the temptation can be strong to control all sides of an argument in service of some perceived public good. No matter how "good" our intentions, we only lose credibility for ourselves and the integrity of our cause when it requires the suppression of competing ideas. There is a reason countries like North Korea and China have walls to keep their citizens from leaving. Closed societies often proclaim the highest of ideals to support trampling on human liberty. But people quickly lose faith in systems that would sacrifice their freedoms on the altar of a social ideal, no matter how lofty. In democratic societies, more subtle methods are employed to suppress the expression of opposing ideas. Yet the effect is still corrosive to discourse, and it still undermines real, organic change.

In recent years, it seems that our society has become more polarized. Discussions and debates and exchange of opinion are the basis of our liberal democracies, and we used to accept different viewpoints as part of healthy development.

In fact, media is considered the fourth pillar of democracy, our guarantee of good objective information and the people's watchdog over the authorities and those in power. The ideal media is always working in-depth to disclose wrongdoing for the common good.

I think it is fair to say that developments in recent years have not followed these principles. The introduction and expansion of new information technologies and social media have certainly given every person a tremendous information base and ways to be heard. But at the same time, these platforms facilitate censorship and information control which likely does more harm than good for whatever agenda is being promoted. Before long, the public resents control and responds with active opposition to an agenda they might have otherwise supported.

Electric vehicles are a good example of this. Increasingly, individuals who initially are neutral to EVs as a transportation option take sides against EVs when they feel they are being forced onto society while their preferred vehicle technology is being attacked. The same is true of ideas. When an idea is forced onto the public while the public's own ideas are suppressed, you replace progress with a backlash, and everyone loses.

Another method of controlling information is to starve it of in-depth and balanced consideration. Too many media companies resort to sensationalizing stories to attract users, giving only headlines, with little or no content to the story. Often there simply isn't time or resources for those reporting to investigate and create a good solid story. Also, software robots scan in real time what people read and how much time they spend reading it, which leads to the creation of more narrow-minded journalism and sensationalistic stories.

Media will cater to their target audience; there simply isn't room for unpopular stories in the mainstream. If we want to find alternative news sources, we must go look for them. The internet has come to stay, and fortunately, in addition to its downsides, it provides a world of information that is only seconds away. Want another analysis of the same issue or story? Well, it is there at your fingertips.

I think the great actor Denzel Washington's reply to a question about fake news unfortunately gives a pretty good description of the information/media landscape we are in: "If you don't read the newspaper you're uninformed, if you do read it, you're misinformed." His answer to

> **News** "If you don't read the newspaper you're uninformed, if you do read it, you're misinformed."

the follow-up question of what to do was "That's a great question. What is the long-term effect of too much information? One of the effects is the need to be first. Not even to be true anymore. So, what a responsibility you all [media] have to tell the truth, not just to be first, to tell the truth. We live in a society now where it's just first, who cares, get it out there. We don't care who it hurts, we don't care who it destroys, we don't care if it's true. Just say it, sell it. Anything you practice you'll get good at. Including BS." [46]

Washington sums it up pretty clearly. More than at any time in history we need to be aware of the information we see, hear, and absorb all around us. We need to be critical. Who is the sender, what is the source of the information, and does it seem balanced? Ask yourself, "Do I really need this?" "Does it make me happier, my life easier, or make me feel better about myself?" "Does this seem likely and reasonable, or do I really want to be part of this?" All these questions, and many more, should be our natural response to any type of information, from "normal" product advertising to information campaigns or propaganda. Always be critical, search different sources for alternative information, and make up your own mind. At the same time, always stay open to new input. In the end, we cannot blame anyone else; we are responsible for our own actions, and we have to dare to be critical of our choices.

Bombarded to stay in the linear system

We are encouraged to spend more, buy more, and discard more only to replace what we have. Let's stop and consider what effect that has. Of course, in the short term it will benefit the companies pushing products on consumers, at the expense of the consumers' bank accounts. Looking at the long-term picture, however, we are sacrificing our finances and our planet to enrich businesses and their marketers, often for temporary personal gain.

I had the honor of connecting with Janez Potočnik, a Slovenian economist and a recognized leader in the circular economy space. He served as European Commissioner for the Environment from 2010 to 2014 and has since worked with global initiatives, including the United Nations Environment Programme (UNEP). We had a good discussion about both the circular economy and overconsumption. Also, as a professor of economics, Janez continues to emphasize the importance of addressing our consumption patterns as the primary issue facing the environment. He believes we are avoiding this crucial issue and focusing on secondary short-term solutions. Throughout his career, he has been a vocal advocate for raising awareness about the significance of environmental concerns in the economic sphere.

Economics is the core driver in politics; there is no way around it. And the application of economics can be a powerful tool in addressing some of the most pressing challenges facing our world today. The rapid growth of the global population and increased interconnectedness of all aspects of society, from the environment to trade and technology, has created a social-ecological space of planetary scope. Our responsibility and awareness have grown, but our actions have not followed. By utilizing economics to address these challenges, we can create sustainable and equitable solutions that will benefit all members of our interconnected global community.

Gross domestic product (GDP), often used by policymakers as a measure of success - a "North Star"- does not accurately reflect the well-being of society. Instead of focusing solely on the economic sector and maximizing market output, policymakers should use a more comprehensive compass that takes into account how well human needs are being met. The overuse of natural resources is a major contributor to issues such as climate change and pollution. A more sustainable approach would be for producers to take responsibility for the entire life cycle of their products, including their end-of-life disposal. This would encourage more sustainable production and consumption practices.

> **GDP** is the total monetary value of all finished goods and services produced within a country's borders in a specific time period.

Here is an example that Januz provided: A refrigerator manufacturer today produces refrigerators that do not last long, and repairs are so costly that it is cheaper to buy new - which creates overconsumption. The manufacturer's responsibility ends when the consumer makes their purchase. If we changed this, the consumer would only lease and pay a fee for the fuel consumed by the appliance, and the producer would be responsible for the entire cycle of the product. This would change the responsibility of the producer and create an incentive to manufacture a longer-lasting and more energy-efficient appliance.

This thought exercise can be adapted to more industries, incentivizing companies to behave responsibly through economics.

The linear mindset emphasizes production capital and rewards it excessively, while ignoring the importance of meeting human needs and valuing the natural environment. This fails to account for the needs of future generations, both in terms of financial debt and the loss of a connection to nature. We have discussed examples of how industry leaders have shifted their thinking to a more long-term view. The circular view is to ask ourselves: "How can the market system be reevaluated to ensure that production capital is appropriately valued, and human needs and nature are given proper consideration and reward?"

In essence, the economy was originally designed to serve human needs, but now it has changed so humans are expected to serve the economy. This has led to a disconnection between humans and nature, with humans being viewed as separate from and in opposition to nature, instead of as integral parts of it. This perspective is unsustainable in the long term, as destroying nature also destroys our own potential future. It is important to change our perspective and recognize that we are a part of nature, not separate from it, and to align our economic systems with this understanding to ensure a sustainable future for all.

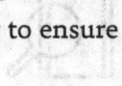

Norway, Oil, and Collaboration

IN NORWAY, non-profit groups, experts, and the media often criticize the oil and gas industries harshly, leaving them out of discussions about sustainability. This approach is like biting the hand that feeds Norway's economy since the oil and gas sectors are a major part of our current income stream.

In 1969, after years of exploration, Philips Petroleum (today ConocoPhillips) found oil offshore what is called Ekofisk, the day before Christmas Eve, as we like to call it in Norway "the little Christmas Eve." And it was truly a gift, because before this discovery Norway was a modest nation economically. Not the poorest and also not among the wealthiest European nations, Norway was a nation rich in resources of fishery, shipping, and agriculture as well as pulp and paper. With the discovery of offshore oil, Norway is now a major producer of gas and oil in the world.[47]

Today, oil and gas exceed half of the total value of Norwegian exports of goods. This makes oil and gas the most important export commodities in the Norwegian economy.[48] Our nation's prominence in oil and gas, paired with our vast hydroelectric resources, has been a cornerstone of our economic success. This dual identity as both an oil nation and a hydro powerhouse has granted Norway a wealth that extends beyond just finances.

Norwegians have done their best to turn that wealth into a more sustainable society for themselves and their children. For instance, the Norwegian government is supporting the development of the world's first full-scale Carbon Capture Sequestration value chain, collaborating closely with giants like Equinor, Shell, and Total. The goal is to lay the groundwork for a European CCS industry. A 2018 SINTEF report highlighted the potential: Europe's CO2 management market might offer 30,000 to 40,000 direct jobs by 2030 and 80,000 to 90,000 by 2050. [49]

> **CCS** refers to a set of technologies and methods designed to capture carbon dioxide emissions from sources like power plants and industrial processes, and store it underground to prevent its release into the atmosphere.

Additionally, the Norwegian government's incentives for battery-powered vehicles, such as exemptions from import taxes, value-added taxes, and highway tolls, have had a significant impact. Now, nearly eighty percent of new cars sold in Norway are battery-powered.[50]

Numerous other initiatives are underway, including electric shipping, the development of hydrogen fuel, and various other projects, all aimed at steering us toward a sustainable society. We are moving forward, and yet we want more progress, now. It's our responsibility, especially in leadership roles, to navigate this legacy responsibly, ensuring a balance between economic growth and environmental sustainability.

> **Hydrogen Fuel** is a zero-emission fuel when burned with oxygen, often used in fuel cells or internal combustion engines to produce electricity or power vehicles.

Understandably, concerns regarding sustainability loom large, but stigmatizing or sidelining part of the energy industries isn't the solution. The complexities of our modern life, deeply interwoven with contributions from these sectors, cannot be denied. Instead of casting the oil and gas sector aside, our focus should be on bridging relationships and seeking inclusive solutions.

Besides, most oil and gas companies have incorporated renewables into their portfolio and are no longer oil and gas companies, but energy companies. This can be reflected at the second largest and most influential gas conference ONS, hosted by The Offshore Northern Seas Foundation (ONS) founded almost 50 years ago (1974) to be the platform for the oil and gas industry.

A new set of leading demands

In 2016, the Norwegian Oil and Gas Association (Offshore Norge) led a national discussion regarding potential new income sources once fossil fuels are depleted. At its center were five millennial students assigned to investigate and hold discussions, research, and provide insights into exactly why the millennium generation's opinions, hopes, and dreams for the future differ so vastly from the oil and gas industry. Millennials are reluctant to work in the oil and gas industry and recruiting new talent has been a challenge.

This conversation gave rise to a major initiative titled "Nye Oljen" ("New Oil"). Emil Yde Aasen was one of five students who travelled across Norway, speaking to nearly 11,000 people, 7,000 of whom were students, arranging workshops at around 40 universities and colleges and visiting over 90 companies. Through social media, the group has reached over 600,000 users on Facebook and their posts have been viewed over 1 million times. Thousands of users have actively engaged with their content.[51]

I was fortunate to interview Emil for this book. He currently holds the position of Business Development Manager at Aker Carbon Capture and loves his work, as it fulfills his mission to create a better planet for future generations. Now, seven years later, he reflected on his experience with the Nye Olien initiative.

Emil explained, "We traveled and conducted focus groups with students in the same age range as us. We laid out the facts, but we did not reveal any solutions. The purpose was to get honest viewpoints and opinions." The foundation of the project was communication where we debated core topics including energy, climate, technology, and welfare. The main topic was whether or not we can replace oil and gas in the future.

Emil went on, "It was important for the dialogue to be with the right age group in open honest conversations. The mandate was to discuss the negatives and positives around oil, gas, wind power, and such, the only criteria being to stick to facts."

One of the exercises that was assigned to the group was to use a card game to draft a new budget for the Norwegian government, considering incomes from various sectors. They had to account for expenses like health care and education, make tough decisions, and incorporate climate solutions.

The biggest revelation was the group's reaction and dynamics.

"The hardest part was realizing how difficult it was to set a budget that balanced all the needs while also thinking about the climate. As a result, many students became emotional and started crying," Emil stated. "What they were facing was how dependent Norway had become on oil and gas. For the first time, they understood the gravity of the situation that the current way of doing things was not sustainable. At the same time, the Norwegian government and society as a whole had built up to a point where the fall would be devastating if there were no alternative solutions to oil."

Emil also noted the disparity between the millennials and the older generation. The report they submitted was a harsh criticism of the oil and gas industry and provided four claims.

- The oil and gas industry sees themselves as a part of the solution and do not admit that they are a part of the problem. *The oil industry has tried to present itself as having the key to opening the door to a better climate. From the perspective of the younger generation, the industry only has the key leading to climate problems.*

- The oil and gas industry does not present a future the millennials want to be a part of. *The Millennials want a future that is based on saving the planet and want the oil and gas industry to take responsibility for moving toward renewable and long-term solutions.*

- The oil and gas industry knows too much to see this generation's point of view. *The report recommended taking the time to see the point of view of the younger generation – they have something to teach the older generation.*

- The oil and gas industry's one-size-fits-all communication just doesn't work. *Emil and his team created the tunnel model to show that the Millennials want a renewable future and for the oil and gas industry to take responsibility for change.*

Currently, we are in the middle of both the best of times and the worst of times. We have AI and technology that will foster getting to the next level and greatly support a new trajectory, but we haven't changed the linear and short-term thinking that undermine a circular economy. The older generation isn't on board with change the way the younger generation is, and the younger generation does not accept this lack of change. Gen-Z has come of age in a time of unprecedented global crises. They are not going to conform to past standards.

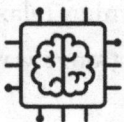

We are in the middle of both the best of times and the worst of times.

The Power of Small Change

The story of four turtles

THIS IS AN OLD, possibly familiar story. The people and the circumstances differ slightly with each storyteller, but the lesson remains the same.

Every Sunday morning, I take a light jog around a park near my home. There's a lake located in one corner of the park. Each time I jog by this lake, I see the same elderly woman sitting at the water's edge with a small metal cage sitting beside her.

This past Sunday my curiosity got the best of me, so I stopped jogging and walked over to her. As I got closer, I realized that the metal cage was in fact a small trap. There were three turtles, unharmed, slowly walking around the base of the trap. She had a fourth turtle in her lap that she was carefully scrubbing with a spongy brush.

"Hello," I said. "I see you here every Sunday morning. If you don't mind my nosiness, I'd love to know what you're doing with these turtles."

She smiled. "I'm cleaning off their shells," she replied. "Anything on a turtle's shell, like algae or scum, reduces the turtle's ability to absorb heat and impedes its ability to swim. It can also corrode and weaken the shell over time."

"Wow! That's really nice of you!" I exclaimed.

She went on: "I spend a couple of hours each Sunday morning, relaxing by this lake and helping these little guys out. It's my own strange way of making a difference."

"But don't most freshwater turtles live their whole lives with algae and scum hanging from their shells?" I asked.

"Yep, sadly, they do," she replied.

I scratched my head. "Well then, don't you think your time could be better spent? I mean, I think your efforts are kind and all, but there are freshwater turtles living in lakes all around the world. And ninety-nine percent of these turtles don't have kind people like you to help them clean off their shells. So, no offense, but how exactly are your localized efforts here truly making a difference?"

The woman giggled aloud. She then looked down at the turtle in her lap, scrubbed off the last piece of algae from its shell, and said, "Sweetie, if this little guy could talk, he'd tell you I just made all the difference in the world."

The moral: You can change the world – maybe not all at once, but one person, one animal, and one good deed at a time. Wake up every morning and pretend that what you do makes a difference. It does.

Small changes of my own

When you pay for something, you certainly want to get the most out of it and not discard, or waste, portions of it. That's Economy, Production, and Common Sense 101.

I consider myself a fairly handy guy, and I often use tools to build and fix things around our home. I used to buy the cheapest tools I could find to save money. I could get electric tools like drills and grinders for as low as twenty dollars. They didn't work very well, but they were cheap, and with some muscle, finesse, pain, and frustration they got the job done. The tools also didn't last long, but since they were so cheap, I could just buy another one when the first one broke.

One time when working on my balcony, I was using one of these cheap drills. It resulted in broken materials, wasted time, and a bloodied hand (perhaps also some colorful language). Finally, I had had enough and went out and bought the best and most expensive drill available. It set me back almost four hundred dollars, twenty times as much as the drills I had been using.

The experience I had using the new tool was an epiphany! The job went smoothly. I finished in far less time than I had anticipated, and the finished result was better than anything I had ever built before. I even had time to enjoy the fruits of my labor afterward, relaxing on my balcony in the sun, refreshed with a beer.

Fifteen years later, I still have the same drill and it works beautifully. It has taken a beating, withstanding hours of use and literally thousands of screws and holes, sometimes even being used as a hammer. I will never again buy cheap tools, because this expensive, quality tool has continued to save me a lot of money, time, and frustration and has given me better results. Better still, by not purchasing "disposable" tools, I have also saved the use of many pounds of copper, steel, aluminum, plastic, and other materials, all contributing to better consumer habits and a more circular economy.

Do we need to change?

We conducted a survey with the ONS foundation of the participants that attended the world's leading energy conference ONS hosted in 2022, gathering more than 60,000 people from 94 countries. The survey provided us with some fascinating insights. [52] One of the most thought-provoking findings was that younger generations are more aware of the need for change and are willing to take action and make personal sacrifices to ensure we provide a better future. However, we cannot expect them to shoulder the burden alone. What can we do to build on the younger generation's existing mindset to spread it more broadly?

In so doing we should avoid simply having a younger generation loudly proclaim old divisive language. If we want to create meaningful change, we need to engage all stakeholders, including industry, in the effort. It's vital that companies prioritize sustainability and incorporate environmentally responsible practices into their operations. This could mean investing in renewable energy sources or adopting circular business models.

Rather than teach our children that the world is divided between evil polluters and righteous environmental warriors, let's also teach them the mindset and the language of finding harmony not just with nature, but also with one another. A circular economy should not only be focused on finding harmony between profits and nature, but also finding harmony between government and industry, people with differing views and experiences. Let's teach the coming generation not to point the finger, but rather ask the question, "How can I be a leader in supporting a more circular society?"

By working together, we can create a future that is sustainable and equitable for all. The younger generation has shown us the way forward, and it's up to us to follow their lead and create a world that we can be proud to pass on to future generations.

There is still so much to do, but that means there are ample opportunities to address the problem in new ways. I've been encouraged in my work with the oil and gas companies to see that the energy industry generally recognizes the need for change. However, many companies are still operating under outdated Key Performance Indicators that prioritize short-term profits over long-term sustainability. As a result, many are reluctant to make the necessary changes. They have begun the recognition phase but are struggling to adopt a new mindset.

During a recent discussion with industry leaders, I asked what steps they could take to address the issue. Unfortunately, their response was predictable. They argued that they couldn't make meaningful changes unless others did so first.

So, we see that the oil and gas industry has not yet been able to make the changes and the risks that we've seen the automobile industry take. What can we do about that? One option is the blaming, finger-wagging, and top-down regulatory approach.

While the youth today are more in line with sustainable living, it is the older generation that is harder to convince. There is a change where the youth are not interested in owning a lot of material possessions and houses. They buy secondhand and at thrift stores. And there are many who are aware of their actions being resourceful and sustainable—but not talking about it.

Still, even as we see this shift, the majority of people in the general population are not willing to make personal sacrifices for circular solutions. And the reason is simple: currently we live in abundance, so there is no dire need to change. In order to make drastic changes, there needs to be a crisis that has a direct impact. To be clear, there is no need to create the perception of a crisis, but rather to inspire change before a crisis is upon us, similar to buying home insurance to safeguard against future issues.

Encourage to Change

> "People don't resist change.
> They resist being changed!"

– Peter Senge, American writer and systems scientist

IF I WERE TO ASK one of my children to clean the kitchen, and then were to come in while he's only halfway through the task and criticize him for half of the kitchen that remains a mess, this would greatly discourage him and cause a level of distrust and resentment. A more positive option is to focus on what he's already accomplished and to help him identify any lessons he's learned along the way. The second option is more likely to help him change his attitude about cleaning and will probably motivate him to finish the job.

Too often, our approach to protecting the environment pits humans against the environment and policymakers against their own constituents. In fact, the media and politicians sometimes benefit by creating division among people and inviting them to take sides against one another. This tactic misses the opportunity to tap into the goodwill of people with varying perspectives. A motivated populace can be a powerful force for change.

Political rhetoric and media negativity create a societal environment of its own which also affects all our lives. Humans need a cleaner planet, but we also need to be able to talk about it without hostility. We can't get to a healthier planet without a healthier, less toxic public discourse on social issues. I hope to inspire policymakers to recognize the powerful trend among the people toward a sustainable mindset and to realize that the public is taking a leadership role in implementing principles of a circular economy on their own. Policymakers have an opportunity to promote policies that support positive trends and use language and policies to unite us rather than divide us.

By tapping into the potential of human goodwill to effect systemic change, we can accomplish much more than through command-and-control approaches alone. Policymakers have a wonderful opportunity to rethink their own strategies and priorities and build a more sustainable and united world for future generations.

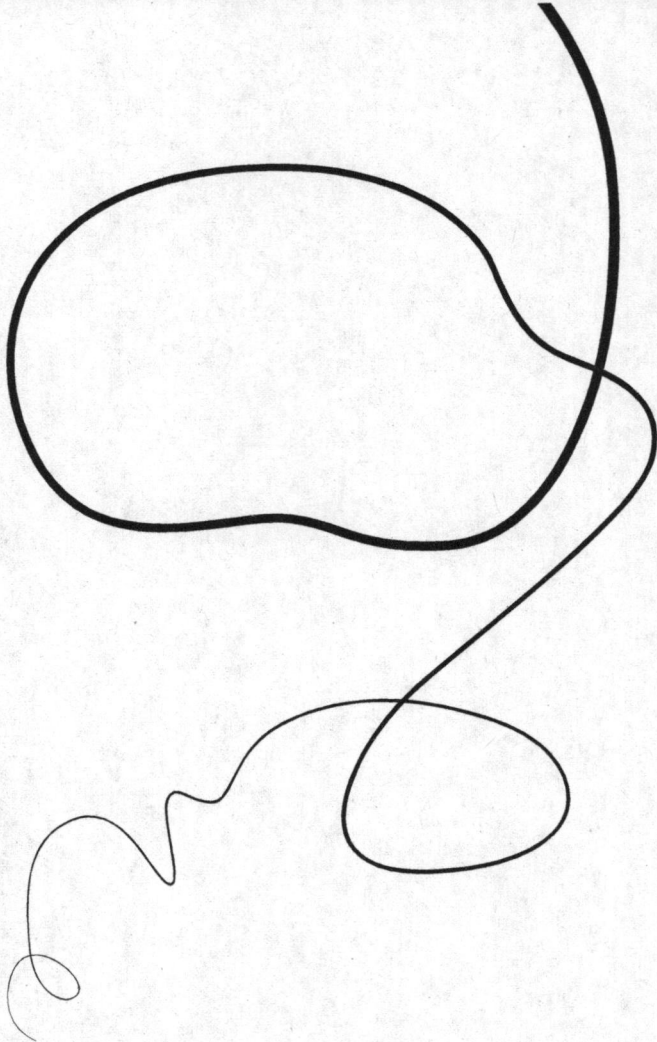

chapter three

we have done it before

We've looked back and analyzed the present, gaining insights into the dimensions of change. Now, we turn our attention to a hopeful roadmap. History shows we have triumphed over environmental challenges, from managing acid rain to reviving the Thames River. This chapter highlights big wins like IKEA's environmental strides and the inspirational stories of individuals who have made a difference. These stories are more than past victories; they are a roadmap for future success. We've navigated these waters before, and with these examples of human innovation and perseverance, we are ready to do it again.

We Have Done It Before

I FIND MY PEACE in nature just a few kilometers away from home at a small, serene lake. It is my escape from the hustle and bustle. This calm and inviting lake is where I wait for a fish to bite, rod in hand – it's perfect for my kind of meditation. But imagine if this sanctuary were spoiled: acidic waters, devoid of fish, littered with plastic. Such a scene is sadly common in many lakes, where the stark reality of environmental neglect replaces the calmness I cherish. The contrast is stark – one, a haven for peaceful meditation and thriving wildlife, the other, a grim reminder of the consequences of pollution and ecological imbalance.

Nature holds immeasurable value, and history shows that when we've gone too far, we've also found ways to correct our course. Take, for instance, the depletion of the ozone layer, mainly caused by chlorofluorocarbons (CFCs) found in things like aerosol spray cans. Back in my high school days, during the 1980s, a shocking discovery was made. Scientists uncovered a massive hole in the ozone layer right above Antarctica. This layer, floating high in the stratosphere, acts as Earth's sunscreen, protecting us from the sun's most dangerous ultraviolet rays. Its thinning posed a threat not just to humans, with a potential spike in skin cancer cases, but also to our oceans' fragile ecosystems.[53]

The chief offenders? Man-made chemicals, primarily CFCs. These compounds, found in everyday items from aerosol sprays to refrigerants, turned malevolent once they ascended to the stratosphere. Sunlight fractured them, releasing chlorine that feasted on the ozone.

The global response was swift, not localized but unified. The looming danger was not to one single country but impacted all countries.

The world gathered, and the Montreal Protocol of 1987 was ratified. Nations came together to take action and vowed to stop the production and use of these ozone-attacking agents. Their goal was lofty, but it underscored a joint vision to restore the ozone layer. [54]

The commitment bore fruit. By 2010, ninety-eight percent of these hazardous chemicals had been eliminated. The ozone layer, once punctured and weakened, began its recovery. With each year, its health improved, and optimism surged. Forecasts now promise that the Northern Hemisphere's ozone will rejuvenate by the 2030s, the Southern Hemisphere by the 2050s, and polar regions by 2060. [55]

The UN Environment Programme asserts that the ozone is expected to return to pre-1980 values by the 2060s over the Antarctic and states, "the healing of the ozone layer is an example of how the world can come together to tackle global challenges."

Together, we solved a global crisis and made the most of our potential to change our course. And we can do it again.

Fishing in the London Thames [56]

Consider London's iconic river, the Thames, which was once so polluted that it was declared biologically dead. By the mid-20th century, this historic waterway had turned into a colossal failure, causing many health and environmental challenges. However, thanks to the determined spirit of a few committed individuals, a massive transformation was set in motion.

In the heart of London's metropolis, a small group of visionaries saw beyond the murky waters. These were not just environmentalists but included forward-thinking entrepreneurs, researchers, and everyday Londoners. They recognized that cleaning up the Thames wasn't just an environmental issue; it was crucial for business. A thriving river would mean new commercial opportunities – from tourism to property development and even recreational businesses.

The business case was clear. Clean water would lift London's global image, enhance property values along the riverbanks, and spur tourism. Recognizing this, they lobbied for radical legislative reforms like the Thames Purification Act. It wasn't just about reducing pollutants; it was about rebranding a significant part of London's identity.

Alongside the legislation, the transformation was backed by data. Researchers, in partnership with businesses, rigorously documented the pollution levels and devised strategies to mitigate them. This wasn't just an academic exercise. It was market research at its core – understanding the problem to chart out sustainable, profitable solutions.

Today, the Thames has witnessed a revival that few thought possible. The return of the salmon, absent for over a century, became symbolic of this turnaround. But it wasn't just nature that benefitted. The Thames transformation led to a flurry of business opportunities – waterfront properties soared in value, tourism spiked, and new recreational ventures found a thriving market.

In essence, the Thames clean-up story isn't merely an environmental triumph. It's a lesson in vision, collaboration, and the lucrative potential of sustainable initiatives. For businesses, it serves as a reminder that sometimes the best commercial opportunities lie in addressing the world's most pressing challenges.

sometimes, the best commercial opportunities lie in addressing the world's most pressing challenges.

Turning the acid rain crisis around

Many parts of Norway and Scandinavia were affected by sulfur emissions from Britain's coal-fired power stations that caused acid rain to fall in Norway's lakes, killing aquatic life. The crux of this crisis lay in atmospheric pollutants, chiefly sulfur dioxide (SO_2) and nitrogen oxides (NOx). These compounds, primarily birthed by industries, power plants, and vehicles, had dire consequences. Lakes transformed into hostile environments, majestic forests became fragile, and even our historical monuments weren't spared from the acidic onslaught.

> **Acid rain** is a form of precipitation with high levels of sulfuric and nitric acids, often resulting from industrial emissions that react with atmospheric water and oxygen.

In the face of adversity, the global community united in its quest for understanding. Researchers spanning from Scandinavia to Europe and North America joined forces. Their collective insights revealed a harsh truth: once airborne, these pollutants were no respecters of national boundaries. [57]

Information and education are power. When the media shared these scientific findings, acid rain swiftly transitioned from being a niche scientific concern to a topic of household discussion. The groundswell of informed public outrage spurred governments into action.

The global response was both swift and strategic. Recognizing the magnitude of public concern, Europe anchored its efforts around the 1979 UNECE Convention on Long-range Transboundary Air Pollution (LRTAP). [58] This initiative laid down clear protocols targeting specific pollutants. Across the Atlantic, the U.S. took a legislative leap with the 1990 Clean Air Act Amendments, pioneering the cap-and-trade system for SO_2, a major contributor to acid rain. [59]

What's truly promising is how nations, acknowledging that air is borderless and in the midst of global crisis, showcased remarkable solidarity. This cooperative spirit led to tangible results, with reduced emissions and a more collaborative international environmental framework.

By the dawn of the 21st century, the results of these efforts were evident. Emissions were on the decline, lakes and forests showed signs of rejuvenation, and architectural marvels were no longer under constant acid siege.

The legacy of acid rain, while diminished, still demands our attention and vigilance. Yet, amid the challenges, there's a silver lining: the episode serves as a testament to human ingenuity and the power of global collaboration. It reminds us that when humanity unites, even the most daunting of environmental challenges can be surmounted.

Gradual Pivots

THE AUTOMOBILE INDUSTRY has been making gradual pivots toward more sustainability. As much as we might want an instant transition to more sustainable options, taking time to ensure products are actually sustainable is worth the wait. And yet, what I find intriguing is that automakers were bringing new technology to market on their own and not as the direct result of a government mandate.

Many automobile executives could not break free from their traditional mindsets when it came to building new advanced technology vehicles. However, Toyota became an early adopter and promoter of hybrid technologies, laying the groundwork for fully electric vehicles. It took an outsider, Elon Musk, to figure out how to make profits with his own environmental ethic and do something truly new. He wanted to see fully electric vehicles (EVs) on the road, and he calculated that there were enough consumers willing and able to pay for a very good EV to make it profitable, if only a very good EV were available.

Around the same time General Motors was preparing to offer a plug-in hybrid vehicle called the Volt, and Nissan was working on the Leaf. While hybrid and natural gas vehicles were a significant improvement over the standard combustion engine, both technologies are still dependent on fossil fuels along with every significant form of transportation on Earth. Whether it is automobiles, long-haul trucks, air travel, rail, or cargo ships, transportation is still largely dependent on fossil fuels.

On the other hand, the Tesla and the Volt would instantly turn the entire electric grid and all its variety into a transportation fuel. Compared with a gallon of gasoline, electricity is cheaper per mile driven, more domestic, more price stable, much more diverse, and more sustainable. Studies showed that an EV powered by a coal plant (the worst-case scenario) still produces fewer emissions per mile driven than a gasoline vehicle.

I interviewed J.J. Brown who was Senator Orrin G. Hatch's energy advisor when Senator Hatch (R, UT) authored the tax credits for hybrids and alternative fuel vehicles in 2005 and then a separate tax credit for plug-in vehicles in 2007.

JJ said, "GM and Tesla weren't being forced by government to take a risk on electric vehicles. Sure, GM had plenty of government pressure to reduce emissions, but no one was telling them how to accomplish that. From a policymaker's perspective Senator Hatch and I were "fossil fuel guys" through and through, but we also had some clean air problems in the Salt Lake Valley, and the senator was very concerned about the national security and economic threat of our dependency on foreign oil."

"When we realized that electricity was the alternative fuel that could best compete with gasoline and diesel on price and that it was 100 percent domestic, that caught our interest. Turning our huge, diverse, efficient, dependable domestic grid into a transportation fuel was a no-brainer from our perspective. Senator Hatch partnered with Senator Cantwell (D, WA), who was a Democrat and was more motivated by climate than Orrin Hatch, but that didn't stop them from joining up and getting the bill passed on the Energy Policy Act of 2005."

"GM and Tesla saw that the public wanted some better alternatives, and they were working on meeting that demand. The public deserves a lot of credit, because in the end consumer interest was really driving this; the development of plug-in vehicles in the US was a ground-up effort. When we saw what GM and Elon Musk were doing and recognized it would make American stronger and cleaner, and we wanted to find ways to accelerate and expand the movement. Elon didn't come asking us for a tax incentive, we went to him and to GM to find ways to enhance what they were already doing."

"GM was focused on a smaller plug-in vehicle that many Americans could afford. Elon Musk on the other hand was going after an expensive roadster built by Lotus. Elon and I were having dinner together at the Monocle, a restaurant right by the Senate, and I asked him why he was building such an expensive and sort of impractical car. He pointed out that he wasn't like GM who could bankroll the Volt with lots of other models. He needed to actually make money on the roadster, and by going for a high-end car, he could charge more for it, and then its high price would help cover the cost of the new technologies. If it were a cheap car, there would be no margin to cover those extra costs. He said his goal was to eventually build models that could hold a family, because he had kids, and he hoped with time he could make more affordable models. But he was banking on the belief that enough customers who wanted a better vehicle could afford one. With a tax credit Hatch and Cantwell were able to help more customers make that choice, but more importantly they were trying to lock in a cleaner, cheaper, and more secure source of transportation fuel."

The automobile industry is moving beyond their own mindsets to find harmony between profits and environmental priorities. As J.J. Brown pointed out, much of the credit for that pivot in priorities for GM, Nissan, and Tesla was their recognition of the changing priorities of their customers, the public. Other automakers were also working on alternative technologies, but they, too, were responding to public demand for something new. As consumers, this a lesson we should keep in mind, especially as we ask ourselves "What can I do?"

The EV story is an example of policymakers getting out of their own linear mindset for policy making. Senators Hatch and Cantwell were responding to a grassroots movement and found a powerful way to support it from the top. A more circular economy can best be supported by a circular policy process. Smart businesses and politicians tend to respond to the demands of the general public. It is always worth letting your priorities be known as a consumer and as a constituent.

Our fear of collapse has led us to create complex and bureaucratic systems, which we believe are essential. But as we become entangled in these webs, we forget the WHY behind our actions. We end up with a plethora of systemic band-aids instead of practical solutions.

Adopting a nature-based mindset, along with circular economy principles, provides a simple solution. By reconnecting with our love and passion for nature, we can ask ourselves a critical question: "How can I bring my actions in line with my love for the planet?" This logical approach grounds us in our values and enables us to make informed decisions that positively impact the environment.

> How can I bring my actions in line with my love for the planet?

We can do it with twenty-five percent or less

Have you ever considered how just a spark, an initial push, or a minor nudge can suddenly change the trajectory of a project, product, or even an entire company?

Imagine you're in a meeting discussing the adoption of a new digital tool in your company. You've got the early adopters on board, but the majority are hesitant. It's easy to get disheartened and think, "This isn't catching on." But here's where the magic happens: research tells us that you might be closer to widespread adoption than you think.

The science of networks and behaviors reveals a fascinating trend.

Once roughly twenty-five percent of a group becomes dedicated to an idea or change, it can trigger a domino effect. That quarter acts as your "committed minority." They don't just like the idea; they live it, advocate for it, and infuse their enthusiasm into their interactions. Their commitment becomes contagious.

Imagine the potential! Say twenty-five percent of your team members are not just using, but championing, that new digital tool. They're showcasing its benefits, streamlining processes, and helping others navigate its features. Before you know it, what was once a tool used by a few becomes a staple for the majority.

For business leaders, this is a goldmine. Instead of focusing solely on overall buy-in from the start, home in on cultivating that committed twenty-five percent. Provide them with the resources, training, and platform to become ambassadors of change. Their energy and dedication can do the heavy lifting, propelling the rest toward the tipping point.

The Thames transformation is an excellent example of this. Once declared "biologically dead" where nothing could survive, London's River Thames was resurrected by an epic clean-up process, but it began with only a few visionaries who saw beyond the immediate challenges. They were the "committed minority" for that cause. Similarly, in our businesses, we need to identify and nurture our twenty-five percent – those individuals who can drive change and push us past the tipping point, turning innovative ideas into mainstream practices.

Let's not forget what Karen O'Brien has taught us, you matter more than you think. We only need a few good humans to change the system, we do not require 100 percent of people to act immediately to adopt widespread circular principles. In fact, research by the Annenberg School of Communications of the University of Pennsylvania demonstrates that we need twenty-five percent of the people or less to create a tipping point of change.[60]

Reflecting on this groundbreaking research, it's intriguing to consider that when about twenty-five percent of a group embraces a novel behavior or norm, a domino effect is set into motion. This committed minority doesn't merely dabble in the new behavior; they advocate, educate, and stand unwaveringly by their convictions.

So, why is this percentage so important?

Minorities that possess unwavering confidence in their beliefs or practices can influence those in the undecided majority. As this influential minority continues to interact and spread its views, undecided individuals, looking for social or functional benefits, also begin to adopt these new beliefs or practices. This forms a cascading effect where the increasing number of adopters further accelerates the pace of adoption, leading to a tipping point.

Organic Movement Goes Mainstream

REFLECTING ON RESEARCH from the University of Pennsylvania in 2018, we see that when about twenty-five percent of a group embraces a novel behavior or norm, a domino effect is set into motion. This committed minority doesn't merely dabble in the new behavior; they advocate, educate, and stand unwaveringly by their convictions. And in the world of organic foods, this phenomenon was prominently observed.

The journey of organic foods, from their humble beginnings to supermarket mainstay, offers a profound illustration of how minority-driven movements can bring about widespread change. As with many social evolutions, it often begins with a committed few who dare to dream differently.

The 1960s and 70s birthed a significant cultural awakening. The "back-to-the-land" movement in the West epitomized this change. Urban dwellers, disillusioned by rampant industrialization, were yearning for simpler, sustainable ways of living. They relocated to the countryside, creating microcosms where organic farming practices flourished.

However, the organic wave wasn't solely propelled by these homesteaders. Literary works played a crucial role too. Rachel Carson's "Silent Spring" (1962) opened many eyes to the perils of pesticides. J.I. Rodale, through his Organic Farming and Gardening magazine, relentlessly championed chemical-free farming.

Amidst this awakening, pioneers in farming sprouted across regions. These weren't large-scale producers but small farmers and cooperatives. They were the leaders in a movement of change, seeing beyond the immediate profits to embrace a holistic approach to agriculture.

The rise of natural food stores in the 70s offered these organic pioneers a platform. These outlets catered to a niche initially: the health-conscious, the environmental enthusiasts, and those exploring alternative diets. But with time, as more consumers tasted and trusted organic, these stores flourished in number and influence.

By the late 1990s and early 2000s, the call for standardized organic practices became louder. Regulations were established, giving consumers clarity and confidence in their organic choices.

Piecing this journey together, it's evident that the organic movement was nudged into mainstream consciousness not by the majority, but by a passionate, persistent minority. They were the early adopters, the advocates, the twenty-five percent who, through consistent efforts, pushed organic foods past their tipping point.

For modern businesses and movements, the lesson is clear: it's not always about achieving immediate, widespread acceptance. Sometimes, the key lies in identifying, nurturing, and empowering that dedicated twenty-five percent. Their conviction, advocacy, and authenticity can tip scales, turning niche ideas into widespread norms.

If we could do it then, we can do it now. In fact, some are doing it already.

1962	1973	1980	1990	2002
Silent Spring Published	Park Slope Food Coop Opens ♥New York	Whole Foods Founded ♥Texas	The Organic Foods Production Act	European Union Organic Certification

Lessons from IKEA

SOME YEARS AGO, I had the opportunity to be a consultant for IKEA. IKEA takes their goal to be circular seriously. Since 2017 IKEA has been designing products to be repurposed, repaired, reused, resold, or recycled with a goal for all products to have circular capabilities by 2030. [61]

During our sessions, they shared with me their long-term perspective and commitment to becoming self-sufficient with renewable energy over the next few years. This impressed me, but what struck me even more was the enthusiasm and pride the employees had when discussing how IKEA used their earnings toward a better and more sustainable society. They recognized the need for change in the ways they sourced their resources and have since implemented a reuse mentality in their future plans, such as exploring alternative materials for their products and finding better ways to repurpose waste. IKEA believes that their own environmental priorities are shared by their customers, and, as a result, profits can be enhanced rather than decreased by the sustainability of their products.

An underlying principle of the emerging circular economy is the recognition that industries can make important changes to their products and means of manufacturing under their own power and that doing so can enhance profits. However, in business, innovation equals risk, and the highest risk is carried by the first movers. If the risk-takers are successful, then the followers will jump in with more confidence.

Consumers and government leaders need to bear in mind the tremendous risk businesses take on when attempting to innovate and shift gears. If the risk doesn't hold the potential for increased profits, there is no incentive to innovate. As with the plug-in tax credit, a financial incentive or rebate provided to consumers who purchase electric vehicles, governments can provide support from the top, but the customer decides if a new endeavor will be rewarded. Success depends upon a satisfied customer. If sustainable products are of poor quality and fail to meet the customer's needs and expectations, no amount of environmental goodwill will matter.

👍 [Success depends on a satisfied customer.]

Thina Margrethe Saltvedt's *Green Pivot*

DR. THINA SALTVEDT is Chief Analyst at the Group Sustainability Nordea Bank, the largest banking group in the Nordic region and a leading spokesperson on sustainability and the circular economy. Thina is setting an example of how one person's spark can ignite others.

Prior to her sustainability career, Thina worked for Nordea over twelve years as an oil analyst before leaving it all behind. Her journey from an oil analyst to an advocate for sustainable finance was not an easy journey, but one that is fueled by an unwavering commitment to a greener future and inspiring others onward.

Having spent two decades as an oil analyst, Thina's *"green pivot"* arrived in waves, prompted by figures like David Attenborough and Al Gore. Their compelling narratives on the dire need for a pivot toward renewable energy prompted Thina to reconsider her professional trajectory. The challenges were tangible: turning toward a career in "sustainable finance" could jeopardize her family's financial standing and put her own job security at risk. But the potential short-term challenges did not compare to her concerns about the long-term implications of a world moving forward without a change.

Thina states, "Personally, I'm worried about nature. When you look at it, we're consuming more and more of what's around us. Animal species are disappearing. Look at the water as well. I come from Vestfold, in a town by the Norwegian coast. Grew up right by the sea and I'm beginning to worry about all the plastic we are beginning to find there."

Thina felt she was seeing the effects of climate change already and how it will impact more and more people. Shortly after grasping the trajectory we were on, Thina left her job and moved into a new position in sustainable finance. This move was not made in fear but rather out of concern and a deep desire to make a change.

I asked Thina if she saw any contradictions between preserving nature and combating climate change.

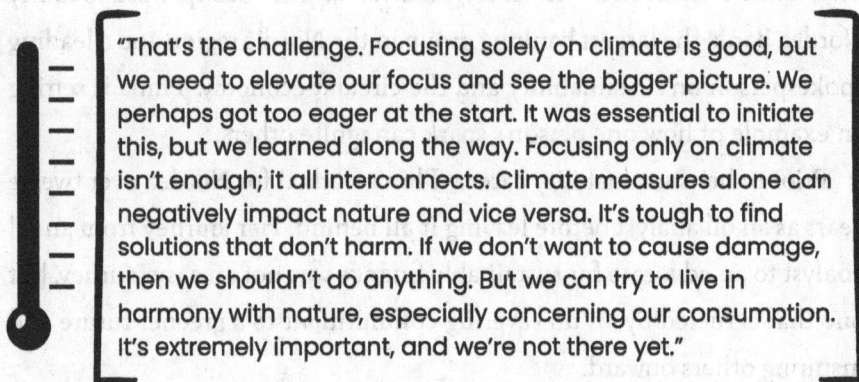

"That's the challenge. Focusing solely on climate is good, but we need to elevate our focus and see the bigger picture. We perhaps got too eager at the start. It was essential to initiate this, but we learned along the way. Focusing only on climate isn't enough; it all interconnects. Climate measures alone can negatively impact nature and vice versa. It's tough to find solutions that don't harm. If we don't want to cause damage, then we shouldn't do anything. But we can try to live in harmony with nature, especially concerning our consumption. It's extremely important, and we're not there yet."

I pressed Thina more on the consumption aspect, as that is what interested me most.

"In wealthy countries, like Norway, consumption is very high. And the impact of our consumption on nature is high too. When you start to see the challenges, you need to understand their root causes. We have a lot of money, right? We want to spend it on something, we have a high standard of living. But the issue is that it has a very negative impact that we need to acknowledge. We need to change our consumption so that it doesn't cause so much damage. We need to reduce our emissions and the footprints we leave behind. I find it exciting to think about what kind of consumption can be sustainable. First, we need to cut down on overall consumption. But then there's also the distribution question. Some parts of the world consume too much while others have nothing. We want to elevate the latter, to achieve a more even distribution of living standards, which would require more resource consumption but in a more balanced way. So, it's a mix of consumption and how can consumption look so it doesn't have such a big footprint? And the other is about a better distribution between different groups."

"I believe that even what an individual does might not have a huge impact, but it does have some effect. Even if the effect is small, it affects the mindset of the collective."

I've looked a bit into the textile industry, and a bit into the construction sector, mostly textiles, though. Again, considering our own clothes and the number of clothes we have. What are they made of? What are the opportunities to reuse those materials? These considerations are incredibly fascinating.

How is it composed, and is it even possible to recycle it? Often, we can't, because we don't even know what's in it. Some materials can be recycled many times, but others are more difficult. Which type of materials should we use more in the future, and which ones should we eliminate from the production process so that materials can be reused, emphasizing circularity."

The good news is that rising living standards do not have to rise with consumption increases. You can still have a good life without all of the stuff.

Being practical is about focusing on the individual level. Taking practical steps toward a more sustainable future there can then trickle up to businesses and government.

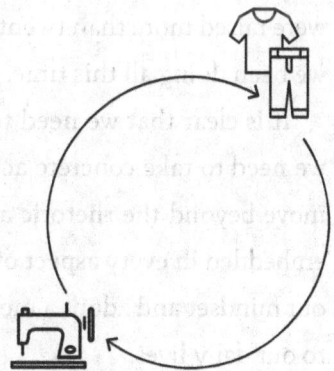

The Power of Collective Change

AS I EMBARKED ON writing this book, I have found it is crucial to engage in dialogue with other individuals in different industries who share similar values and perspectives. Through these conversations, I have gained valuable insights and knowledge that have been eye-opening. Despite being involved in this industry for years and attending various forums with the same individuals who share the same passion for sustainability, I realized that we are often just preaching to the choir.

Recently, I had the opportunity to speak with Andrew Winston, an author and speaker who has been deeply invested in sustainability for over two decades, from a business and environmental perspective. Our conversation was candid and intriguing, and we both came to the realization that the issues we are discussing today are the same ones that were raised more than twenty years ago. This begs the question: what have we been doing all this time, and why has so little changed?

It is clear that we need to do more than just talk about sustainability; we need to take concrete actions and make tangible changes. We need to move beyond the rhetoric and embrace a culture of sustainability that is embedded in every aspect of our lives. This means that we need to change our mindset and adopt a more resourceful, mindful, and holistic approach to our daily lives.

As we move forward, we need to prioritize sustainability as a core business value and ensure that it is incorporated into every aspect of our decision-making processes. We must recognize that our actions have a direct impact on the environment and the communities in which we operate, and we need to take responsibility for our actions.

To truly make a difference in our efforts to promote sustainability through a circular economy and nature-based mindset, it's not enough to focus solely on the what and why of these concepts. The most critical aspect is WHO - the people we need to reach and engage. For too long, we've been speaking to a narrow audience, using technical jargon to which many cannot relate. As a result, we've failed to educate the masses, the real influencers and users who hold the power to drive change.

> The most critical aspect is **WHO** - the people we need to reach and engage with.

To create a sustainable future, we must involve and educate everyone, especially the end-users, as they wield the biggest significant influence. However, we need to recognize that the topics of the circular and nature-based economy can often be complex and difficult to understand. To achieve real change, we must find ways to make these issues relatable to everyone. We need to communicate and present information in a way that fosters understanding and encourages a change in mindset.

Education is key. We need to incorporate these concepts into our schools and universities, teaching them on the same level as math and reading. We need to ensure that these concepts are accessible to everyone, regardless of their background or socioeconomic status. By educating everyone about the benefits and importance of circular and nature-based economies, we can foster a collective understanding and mindset that will drive us toward a sustainable future.

Furthermore, we must not limit these concepts to certain circles or communities. It is essential to break down the barriers that exist between different groups of people and sectors of society. Only by working together can we create real change that benefits everyone. We need to involve businesses, governments, NGOs, and individuals from all walks of life in the conversation and decision-making process.

For us to achieve a sustainable future, we must ensure that the concepts of circular and nature economy are accessible, relatable, and understandable to everyone. Finding the language and message that resonates with the populace is the first step. We must work together to break down the barriers that exist between different groups of people and sectors of society.

During my conversation with Walter Stahel, a Swiss architect and a leading authority on circular economy, he provided me with a fresh perspective on how we can raise awareness among not only ourselves, but also manufacturers and legislators. Stahel emphasized the importance of action rather than simply talking about change. One of the biggest obstacles to implementing new policies and embracing a circular economy is often the bottom line and profitability. Companies are reluctant to uproot and change production methods that have been ingrained in our systems and mindset for centuries.

However, Stahel argues that by turning our focus to a circular economy, we can create new revenue streams and increase profitability. Rather than relying solely on traditional linear models of production and consumption, we can adopt more sustainable practices that generate value from secondary use materials and extend the life of products. This approach not only benefits the environment but also creates new opportunities for innovation and growth.

To overcome the resistance to change, we need to work together and find ways to incentivize companies to adopt circular economy principles. This may involve introducing regulations or tax incentives that reward sustainable practices and penalize wasteful ones. It may also involve educating consumers and encouraging them to support companies that prioritize sustainability.

It will take a concerted effort from all stakeholders to create a more sustainable future. By embracing a circular economy, we can challenge the status quo and drive real change toward a more resilient and equitable world.

Walter advocates for a shift in focus. He suggests that instead of just concentrating on quarterly reports, there should be more emphasis on Risk Management and Liability. Given that investors tend to shy away from risk, highlighting the aspect of liability could be a more effective way to capture their attention. Responsibility needs to go into the sustainability report, while liability needs to go into the financial report. The financial report is what the investors looking at. By learning to use these tools of the economy, we can put liability back on the producer/manufacturer as an inducement for positive change in order to maintain their investor pool. If a company wants to innovate and make real changes toward sustainability but can't find the funding in a short-term profit environment, a good liability description of a status quo scenario in a changing consumer/customer base can be a decisive move in securing the necessary understanding and funding.

Liability refers to the legal responsibility of a company for debts, obligations, or potential legal judgments that may arise in the course of its operations.

CHAPTER FOUR

solutions

So, what do we do now?

This chapter will explore various ideas, theories, and approaches already in use aimed at creating a more circular economy. It will cover concepts dating back as far as the 1980's, all the way to the up and coming ideas of today.

Design Is the Way: My Interview with Ian Peterman [62]

"Design creates culture.
Culture shapes values.
Values determines the future."

-Robert L. Peters, Canadian Graphic Designer and Educator

DESIGN CONSTRICTS and creates guidelines. It is the solution to implementing principles of the circular economy. The Montreal Design Declaration, which represents over 700 professional associations, design schools and stakeholders, defines design as "the application of intent: the process through which we create the material, spatial, visual and experiential environments." [63]

Design is more than the act of making something look nice; it should be a strategic approach that influences and drives everything – from the actual products to the spaces we operate in and the experiences we deliver. The Declaration proclaims the potential of design to achieve global economic, social, environmental, and cultural objectives and includes a dramatic call to action to professionals, educators, and governments as well as a list of proposed projects. [64]

To become truly circular, I realized, we would need to go up the value chain to the start of everything, design. I quickly saw that it can be a complex matter but also, in some ways, so simple. Anyone and everyone can be more *circular* than we are today, from me, as a single individual or household, to gigantic international corporations. I started seeing that our ability, or rather need, to be circular had been lost somewhere along the way in the last century.

The design phase of a product in development holds critical importance that is often overlooked. **According to the EU Science Hub, "over 80% of all product-related environmental impacts are determined during the design phase of a product."**[65] Designers have a crucial role in determining the sustainability and environmental footprint of the products we develop and use.[66]

> "over 80% of all product-related environmental impacts are determined during the design phase of a product."

80% Design

Why such a big percentage at the upfront development phase?
During the design phase, choices are made about materials, manufacturing processes, durability, and end-of-use considerations. These decisions set the framework and guidance for the product's lifecycle and influence factors such as sourcing the materials, energy use, waste management, recycling, or reuse. By focusing on sustainable design principles from the beginning, companies can drastically reduce the negative environmental consequences associated with their products.

Circular design isn't just good for the environment; it's smart business. Today people want eco-friendly products, and companies that deliver on this promise meet a growing demand. By focusing on circular design, businesses not only help the planet but also stand out in their industry.

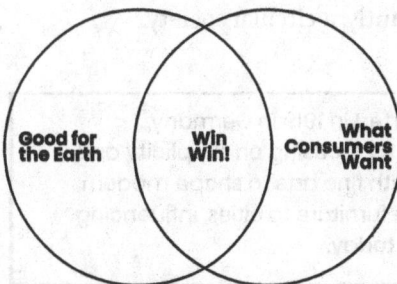

Good for the Earth — Win Win! — What Consumers Want

In a world where resource scarcity, decreasing natural areas, and declining biodiversity are pressing concerns, the design phase presents a unique chance for innovation and positive change. By integrating sustainability and circularity into design processes, businesses can achieve a double win: reducing their ecological footprint while at the same time meeting the demands of consumers and strengthening brand reputation. I see a future where the circular mindset has borne fruit for so many organizations that the old linear approach will be considered obsolete and undesirable.

I had the privilege of interviewing one of the foremost thinkers on Conscious Design, Ian Peterman. He states,

> **"We are all designers.** Design is about creating the limits that fit the strategy. Design is the purposeful creation and arrangement of elements to achieve a specific goal or solve a problem aesthetically and functionally."

Conscious Design is the philosophy Ian uses at his design firm, the Peterman Design Firm. His book book, *Conscious Design*,[67] helps people look at the world and design in a more conscious way. Ian prioritizes restorative, sustainable, and inclusive values to build a legacy of positive impact for his client's brands. His firm specializes in developing and commercializing products and offers branding and marketing for clients' missions and circular products and projects. Ian Peterman, along with his wife Jessica Peterman, developed the idea of Conscious Design as a blueprint to help other designers create for the world we want to live in, not just the one we live in now. Now, it's the foundation of the Conscious DesignHaus, a non-profit that takes the best of the Bauhaus movement and infuses modern and circular concepts to bring our current generation forward toward a fully circular economy and, even more importantly, a circular society.

> **The Bauhaus movement**, started in 1919 in Germany, revolutionized art and design by focusing on simplicity and practicality, blending crafts with fine arts to shape modern architecture and design, from furniture to cities, influencing how we make and see things today.

The Peterman Conscious Design method is built on four key pillars:

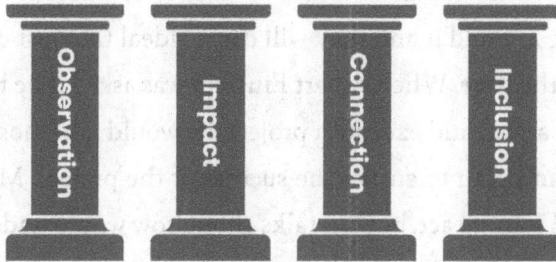

Observation | Impact | Connection | Inclusion

Each product must be developed with the core beliefs of both the creators and the users, creating a shared story considering not only the user but everyone who comes in contact with the product from start to finish— and performing all of this with collaboration at its center. Creating truly conscious and circular products requires starting in the design phase, hence Conscious Design as a design thinking process.

Dialogue is of primary importance when initiating any project. Truly understanding what the problem is to be solved and how to solve it must come before you begin to architect a design.

Talking to Ian, I realized that **we often neglect the most important pillar: Observation.**

The other pillars of impact, connection and inclusion, are fairly self-explanatory, but observation took me by surprise and also made me realize how important it is to observe and ask questions before starting a project.

Observation defined

"If I had an hour to solve a problem, I'd spend 55 minutes thinking about the problem and five minutes thinking about solutions."

—ALBERT EINSTEIN

Projects fail due to a lack of observation and time to plan. Review all the possibilities of what can go wrong. We rush to the execution phase too often, creating a "build it and they will come" ideal that just doesn't really work most of the time. When Albert Einstein was asked if he had only one hour to create a plan and execute a project, he would take most of the time on strategies and plan to ensure the success of the project. Most of us are impatient and want to act, but Ian talks about how we are underestimating the potential of observing and spending more time in dialogue, asking questions, planning, researching, and designing, before trying to produce, sell, or market a product. By taking time to plan, big questions can be answered first, ones that can truly shape the entire project.

When starting a project, take time to observe. Ask. Examine the past successes and failures. The key is to truly understand the pain and problems of your potential users/customers, develop a solution and test, assess, and test again to ensure its viability and that it fills the need.

"In our fast-paced society, we often rush into developing business solutions without taking a moment to truly assess our surroundings. This is likely why roughly 80% of startups and products fail," states Ian.

Projects are more likely to succeed if the time is taken to observe and understand the starting point and the direction in which the project needs to head.

The observation phase gives you time to compile some key data points:

- Will you be dealing with manufacturing?
- Will you have agents for sales?
- What does the customer's journey look like?
- Should this be disposable or permanent?
- What is truly the most sustainable option for this product?

Study companies that excel in this aspect and learn from any unfavorable outcomes and experiences, make necessary adjustments. Taking these steps can be the difference between bankruptcy and success.

The key with observation is to stay slow and steady and ensure you are on the right track. Analyzing both successful and unsuccessful companies and learning from bad experiences can lead to adjustments that enhance the longevity of your brand.

Ian concludes, "It's important to note how important questions are. Asking the right question should lead to more questions, not just a singular answer, especially at the beginning of trying to create an amazing solution for a user."

Sustainability is not the solution

What is surprising is that, while many work so hard to be sustainable, the idea of sustainability as a selling point is not enough to drive economic growth. People typically make purchases for one of two reasons: to fulfill a specific need or to satisfy an emotional desire. While the appeal of sustainability is genuine, there's a growing saturation of sustainable products. It's no longer enough to stand out simply by being sustainable. Companies need to create products that effectively solve problems and provide enjoyable experiences, with sustainability as a core component and a part of their mission.

Ian told me about how Equo, a sustainable single use product brand, had launched various sustainable straw options, including those made from coffee grounds, sugar cane, and even grass. What they discovered was that the user's first priority was to have a functional straw, and a straw that would not affect the flavor of their drink. They found certain options, such as grass straws, were not well received because they flavored everything to taste like grass. People wanted to be sustainable and use a biodegradable straw, but the product's first requirement was at least as good an experience as a plastic straw, which meant it couldn't change the drinks flavor. If it couldn't work right, it was not a successful product. A secondary and yet essential quality is that the product be sustainable.

"Selling a sustainable product that effectively addresses a problem is ideal. If you have the most perfect sustainable product, but no one ever buys it, you've actually made the most unsustainable product in the world, because it will never make a positive impact and will have instead wasted resources of everyone involved."

Thus, the coffee and grass straws developed by the company Equo[68] were in fact useless, as people do not want straws to give an aftertaste of coffee or grass flavor when drinking something.

Yes, we want sustainable, but it needs to be practical.

Practical means not creating new problems to overcome.

People recognize environmental issues, but sustainability or circularity are not stand-alone selling points. A product must first provide clear benefits and not diminish its useful experience; that is, a sustainable straw should not alter the taste of the beverage.

People buy products that solve problems, whatever the product. Solve this with sustainability at its core.

The key is to create a product that people want.

What do people want?

Vision, mission, solving a problem, and beautiful design sell. It is the reason that engineers flock to companies like Tesla because they are innovating, creating products of the highest excellence, and are also part of a grander vision, the vision to improve life on the planet with aesthetically pleasing design. Tesla checks all the boxes. There have been several other electric

☐ **Vision**
☐ **Mission**
☐ **Beautiful Design**

vehicles, including quite a few back in the early 1900's. However, every electric car made in recent history failed, because it never captured the imagination. As they say, sexy sells, and the Tesla Roadster was considered a *good looking* car when it was released. Tesla made electric look good and captured the hearts of people who would have never been caught dead buying a Chevy Volt.

There was another electric car on the market that you have probably not heard of and it was called Th!nk, an electric city car manufactured by Norwegian automaker Think Global that many thought had a rosy future only to end production in 2012.

It was an electric city car that produced its first car in 2000 with the support of the Ford Company but was not able to create enough interest. The explanation seemed to be that it was too early, and people were not ready for an electric car.

Then, in 2008, Th!nk developed strong partnership with Valmet Automotive, a company with deep pockets thanks to the major shareholder, TESI, the Finnish state-owned investment company with solid experience in the EV space. It seemed go well as Th!nk in 2011 was among the five electric cars globally that passed the test of being considered a respectable choice and had undergone crash testing, achieved mass production, and received highway certification. But people were not buying Th!nk. Instead, it went out of the business with the clear leader being Tesla.

Why?

Consumers are complex and need more than just a green label to motivate a major purchase. While Th!nk prioritized sustainability, it seemed to neglect the importance of design and usability. To me, the car didn't resonate—it felt too small to be practical. Even though it was electric, it lacked the captivating quality.

On the other hand, the Tesla Roadster, with its sleek aesthetics, reminded me of the allure that Apple's iPod, iPad, and iPhone brought to the table. Design plays a crucial role—it dictates whether people are drawn to a product.

> ## Developing a sustainable product simply for the sake of sustainability is not sustainable.

Big companies stuck in a linear world

The giant conglomerates and established corporations are struggling to adjust to new consumer expectation as many are set in a linear thought pattern, and in many cases, there has not been a significant change in their approach over the past decades -- their colossal structures, marked by deep-seated corporate cultures and compartmentalized departments, have made them resistant to rapid change.

Ian Peterman, a seasoned player in the corporate world, recalls one of his first jobs working as an engineer at a prominent printer producing company. He was part of a dedicated team that conducted the destructive testing of large office printers and was responsible for testing and dismantling prototypes to assess possible design flaws. The challenge was that they were one of the final checkpoints before the product went to market. Often, they identified structural issues that were "known issues" by his team, but these flaws kept getting introduced at an earlier stage, because that information never made it back to the first level of design.

As Ian reflected, traditional corporate *silos* cost time and resources. If the testing team had been collaborating from the outset with the design team and working with other teams, such as marketing and sales, they would have prevented inefficiencies and significant waste, particularly in plastics and electronics. Instead, the teams were in *silos*, imprisoned in rigid structures limiting internal collaboration and limiting growth for the company. This experience is one of the reasons Ian Peterman created the Conscious DesignHaus, to help break down silos to improve efficiency and to utilize great design to achieve circularity by creating a better flow of information flowing down to the individual level.

A **silo** refers to a system, process, or department that operates in isolation from others, often leading to a lack of communication and collaboration within an organization.

The way of the future: startups

Startups, with their lean structures and nimble cultures, are spearheading change. They are the future. Ian is confident that startups will lead the Circular revolution. Their greatest selling point is not the features of the product but rather the mission and vision that inspires sustainability, diversity, and a promise to leave the world a better place.

Today, people seek a clear vision and a brand promise. They are demanding more eco-friendly products and ethical practices; sustainability is no longer just an optional marketing point; it's becoming an expectation.

Startups, not bound by traditional practices, can more easily incorporate sustainability from the outset. But they must be careful. More than we want, small companies grow large and begin to take on silos. It's only with great vigilance and culture creation that these silos can be kept away.

On the other hand, for the established giants changing to be more sustainable in action remains a challenge. This is, primarily because sustainability is not part of their foundational culture and they are so heavily invested in yesterday's products and way of doing things.

However, a few leaders among the larger brands are beginning to make up that twenty-five percent committed minority. Brands like Apple have been progressing toward zero waste for decades. Luxury car brands like Bentley and Rolls Royce, once the bastions of combustion engines, are now embracing the electric revolution. The very fact that these luxury brands are making the transition signifies the industry's acknowledgment of sustainability as more than just a fleeting trend.

Now, consider the role of design in this ever-changing landscape. The temptation for companies is to be single focused and frantic and find a fast one-sided solution, instead of being deliberate in assessing the right strategy to move forward.

"To sprint, one must first know which direction to head toward. Fast fashion, for instance, has led to immense waste. But platforms like Plato's Closet are turning this around by focusing on second-hand products, making fast fashion more sustainable. It's about the actual use of a product, its longevity, and its eventual environmental impact."

But the future of design is not just about sustainability. The challenge is to solve both practical and emotional problems for the consumer. The product must be sustainable, yet this alone isn't a selling point anymore. The real challenge lies in integrating sustainability seamlessly, so the consumer barely notices it.

Concluding this narrative of change is the reality of the circular economy. As Ian puts it, the large corporations have turned to a strategy of acquisition over innovation. Rather than delving into R&D, they now wait for startups to innovate and then buy them out. It's a strategy that, unintentionally, is fast-tracking our transformation toward a circular economy.

Startups, by virtue of their size and agility, are more attuned to modern problems and solutions. And when these startups get bought and integrated into larger companies, their innovations reach a broader audience at a much-accelerated pace.

Janez Potočnik supports Ian's argument: startups are shaping the future. Instead of only relying on product features, these new entrants are focusing on impactful missions, often related to sustainability or fair trade.

We're seeing startups gain ground against long-established brands, not necessarily because they have better products, but because they connect with consumers on deeper personal values. This trend is amplified by platforms like Kickstarter, where people back not just products, but missions and visions they believe in.

What this essentially underscores is the immense interconnectedness of it all - our economy, society, environment, and the choices we make. We are witnessing a dynamic shift where every player, from the smallest startup to the biggest corporations, plays an important role in crafting a sustainable future. All we need to ensure is that we are dancing to the right tune.

Ian concludes, "We get to live on this planet and it's easy to think, "it's worked this long, why change it now?" But what if we cannot continue as we have? What about the finite resources that drive the comforts and necessities of modern life? And what about all the impractical solutions to these problems that are problems in and of themselves?

Stories of Inspiration

IT IS EASY TO THINK that we are not making progress, and I hope that I have demonstrated in this book that many things are going positively well. In this section, I want to highlight some organizations that are moving the needle of progress in the right direction.

Case study #1 - circularity can simplify

When I challenged creative director Nils-Petter Wedege to build a 100 percent regenerative exhibit stand for RENAS about the circular economy at the ONS conference in 2022, he took on the challenge even though he was unsure how to make it work. My team and I created a framework of what circular meant: to ensure all of the stand's parts would last as long as possible in the cycle of use. The main focal point of the stand was the circular message and a meeting place to dialogue, entertain, and educate on the importance of the circular economy. We were inspired by nature, raw materials, and human beings. Our goal was to create a stand that would last for ten years at the end of which all of the pieces could be reused or recycled.

We asked ourselves, "How can we create a stand that embodies circularity in its message and is reflected in all of our actions?"

Nils Petter, the creative director at Fabel Media, a Norwegian creative agency, found that our guidelines greatly simplified his job. As he reflected, "I can't believe that we managed to build something so aesthetic from things that have been used before. And what is great about this is that it gets new life here – some of them we bought, some of them were given and some we have borrowed. **When you start by thinking circular, things** become easy, it becomes practical, and that is what we want to do here. Let's get Practical!"

The design phase of a product in development holds critical importance that is often overlooked. According to the EU Science Hub, "over 80% of all product-related environmental impacts are determined during the design phase of a product." Designers play a crucial role in determining the sustainability and environmental footprint of the products we develop and use.

Circular design isn't just good for the environment; it's smart business. All of this is just to say that when you think circular from the very beginning and spend extra time to plan, your life and projects actually become simpler.

#2 HOKA – less is more

A small company with the heart of a start-up is outpacing established shoe companies with a vision, mission, brand, and high-performance shoes.

Founded in 2009, HOKA is a footwear brand with the vision to design running shoes that not only are kind to the human body and deliver world-class performance but also commit to saying yes to less waste, less plastic, and fewer trees.

In just four years, Deckers, the force behind Ugg, acquired HOKA. A few years later, HOKA now accounts for an impressive 36 percent of Deckers' revenue, up from 21 percent only two years earlier. By 2022, HOKA had surpassed a billion dollars in sales.

Not only does HOKA have a strong *why*, at the heart of their products is a circular design, ensuring minimalism and sustainability, while not compromising on performance. Their new shoe Restore TC, for example, is marketed as: "Maximal Comfort. Minimal Materials: A progressive slip-on designed with the circular economy in mind, Restore TC is engineered from minimal materials and employs a simple, three-part construction." [69]

HOKA Mission Statement

We all choose our own way to explore this amazing planet we live on. Some of us run. Some wander. And others all out race. But we all call here, home.

At HOKA, we know home needs protecting.

That's why we're on a mission to team up and — in big and small ways — to reduce our impact. As we look forward — for more ways to do better, we're saying Yes to Less.

Yes, less unwanted materials

Over 97% of our footwear styles contain at least one preferred material (a recycled, renewed or naturally sourced material).

Yes, less petrol-based plastic

55% of all co-polyester fibers in footwear and 70% in apparel and accessories will come from renewable or post-consumer/industrial resources by 2030.

Yes, less trees

HOKA's recycled paper efforts have saved over 802,000 trees since 2016.

Yes, less waste

Our California distribution center will be a zero-waste facility by the end of 2023.

Yes, less carbon emissions

Our goal is to reduce energy usage in our footwear by 25% per shoe by 2030.

Yes, less water

We've committed to reducing water usage at HOKA footwear by 20% by 2030.

What sets HOKA apart isn't just its rapid growth but its underlying mission. HOKA's mission transcends footwear. The alignment of high-quality product design, compelling mission, and grasp of the people's pulse has positioned HOKA as not just a footwear brand, but as a disruptor set to redefine the industry. Former CEO American Wendy Yang, the first female president of a running brand stated in 2019, "We're a 10-year-old brand that started from ground zero... If we can continue doing what we're doing, we can get to half a billion dollars per year."[70]

#3 Arizona's green leap forward

In Arizona, rapid expansion isn't just a challenge—it's an opportunity. Vice Mayor Solange Whitehead of Scottsdale is turning the tide, showing that eco-friendly policies can also fuel economic growth. Her goal is to create eco-friendly living areas that support the state's growing population without damaging the environment.

During her tenure, Solange saw the rise of green projects in Arizona as a step in the right direction. Still, she believed this was not enough because these innovative efforts often only benefited a few, while many Arizonians were burdened with high utility bills due to inefficient housing.

To address this, Solange initiated community discussions to find win-win solutions when discussing water conservation and eco-friendly policies. This approach kick-started conversations about the practical benefits of sustainability for everyday residents.

Under her leadership, Scottsdale didn't just join the green movement; the city led the way by becoming the first in the state and one of only a few nationwide to adopt mandatory 'green' building code requirements. The move, surprisingly supported by a Republican-majority council, reflects Scottsdale's deep-rooted tradition in conservation that makes economic sense.

What is the result of adopting the 2021 edition of the International

Energy Construction Code (IECC) and the International Green Construction Code (IgCC) as mandatory codes?

The new energy code (IECC) applies to new residential and commercial buildings, resulting in lower energy use, cost savings, thermal comfort, and reduced environmental impacts. [71]Scottsdale's updates are a model of efficiency, including better insulation in homes, LED lighting, smart lighting controls, and automatic shut-offs for outdoor lights. [72]They're also future-proofing homes with electric vehicle charging infrastructure and solar-ready rooftops. This isn't just about meeting today's needs—it's about preparing for tomorrow.

The result for the residents is not just greener surroundings but substantial savings. The numbers speak for themselves: a 10.6 percent savings in energy costs and a 10.2 percent reduction in greenhouse gas emissions compared to 2018 standards.

When asked what the ingredient for success is, Whitehead stated that it was to find what is in it for the public. By showcasing the advantages of being a conservationist, she could stave off the special interest groups that wanted to keep the status quo and instead have Scottsdale lead the nation.

#4 The Lego way: building play and creativity

> The fact that you can take LEGO bricks from thirty years ago.
> and they still snap together with the same new LEGO brick that comes out,
> I mean what type of product can span generations like that,
> there is something really special to it.
>
> -- Nathan Sawaya, Brick Artist

Lego holds a special place in my heart. As a child, I spent hours crafting castles and bridges, engaging in imaginative war games with my friends.

Then, as we grew older, video games took the spotlight, gradually replacing Lego. Later, I saw my own son engrossed in the same Lego set, albeit with a few scratches here and there. Despite the changes, one thing remained constant: Lego's ability to fuel creativity and imagination.

Lego is a great example of the circular economy principles of reusing building to last.

In business of improving our planet it is easy to be negative and lose sight of the positive, and yet play makes the world go around. Play inspires creativity and provides greater opportunity for innovation, but we forget to play.

What I found out when working on this book is that the Lego Foundation has a section called the Lego to help build creativity.

We might want to bring out the Lego box at work and play, laughing and working together to build and tear down buildings, bridges and other great creations thus allowing great ideas to flow.

Play does increase innovation and boost productivity, as Tracy Brower, PhD, Senior Contributor for Forbes Magazine states, "Increase productivity 20%—who doesn't want that? In a new study by Brigham Young University, teams that played a collaborative (video) game together for just 45 minutes were able to increase their productivity on a task by 20%." [73]

She continues to state it is not just playing video games that can hack our productivity and boost our bottom-line. According to Dr. Brower, play in general increases innovation, unites teams' members, and allows us to let our stress out.

I believe that doing this kind of exercise will help find the good, sustainable, nature-based solutions.

> ## The Linear consequence
>
> We can't ignore the tremendous pull that the linear economy has on major industries such as Lego. In recent years, Lego has recognized that once a child purchases a set of Lego building blocks, they will last forever, and in some ways, they have lost a customer. For that reason, the company has come out with a whole host of Lego packages based on Star Wars, on Harry Potter, on superheroes, and other popular media products. Now instead of Legos being the generic shapes that force children to use their own imagination, it's the designers who are creating and the customers are simply assembling the Legos according to instructions. Playing with Legos has shifted into model building, and then those Lego pieces are not useful to be used to create anything else. As long as the collector keeps the Lego model on his or her shelf, that could be considered a long-term use. I don't blame Legos for finding ways to build repeat customers, but I would encourage them to bring back creativity into their products and to find new ways to bring circularity into their use of resources. A Lego-specific recycling program for customers who want to clear their shelf space of their old Lego models is just one idea they could employ.

Challenge: linear thinking lingers

When I interviewed Ian Peterman, he was primarily working with companies on slow change. He stated, "We are in a new future, and being sustainable is a commodity. All companies are required to show their green vision and way of doing things. The mission and vision of any company is the greatest differentiator and the way to create a healthy and wealthy company."

Silo culture is a byproduct of the linear economy. Ian shows companies that the new way to thrive is to be collaborative. We have outgrown siloed thinking, and it is destructive for companies today.

Large organizations are making efforts to make substantial changes toward sustainability. One such company is Ralph Lauren, which is set to become 100 percent sustainable in five years. In a conversation with the Head of Sustainability, we discussed how Ralph Lauren hopes to accomplish its goal.

To embark on this transformation, Ralph Lauren had to establish a new team and initiate a pilot program. It's not enough to just say, "Let's do everything sustainably from now on." They needed to demonstrate that sustainability could be profitable, showcase their ability to execute the plan, secure buy-in from shareholders, and secure the necessary funds to implement the changes.

Words Matter

> I have seen how effective language attached to policies that are mainstream and delivered by people who are passionate and effective can change the course of history.

–Frank Luntz

AFTER HEARING DR. FRANK LUNTZ speak at a conference in Norway about how the right words can change the direction of society, my eyes were opened to the power our word choices truly have. Until then, I knew words were important for communication, but I thought their importance was merely to express ideas. I learned from Frank that how we phrase something can change the perception of the word and its meaning. Words don't merely explain meanings; they shape perceptions, evoke emotions, and have the potential to redefine public discourse.

Dr. Frank Luntz, a leading political strategist, pollster, and bestselling author of "Words Matter," entered the political scene shortly after earning his PhD from Oxford. He served as a pollster for presidential candidate Ross Perot. The success of Perot's campaign divided the conservative voting bloc, resulting in the victory of Democratic candidate Bill Clinton..

What few may know is that the word "Climate Change" was coined by Frank Luntz in 2001 in a memo addressed to President George W. Bush and the Republicans. Global warming had gotten a bad reputation, and it did not help when Vice President Al Gore held hearings in Congress that had to be canceled due to winter storms. Global warming wasn't seen as accurate and was mocked by many Americans. Frank suggested using

"Climate Change" to better fit the Republican agenda of conservation. This term felt less urgent than "global warming" and became widely used.

In August 2019, I was introduced to Frank, when I was given the opportunity to sponsor his visit to Norway as the keynote speaker at the conference "The Art of Framing Sustainability." This event was organized by Torund Bryhn, a researcher on the climate technology CCS and Language, in collaboration with BI Norwegian Business School's Centre for Corporate Communication and Centre for Green Growth. The goal was to identify language that could spur action for sustainability. We at RENAS sponsored this event, eager to learn how to inspire people to embrace the principles of the circular economy.

What intrigued me was Frank's regret over coining the term "climate change." The reason he was invited to speak was due to a statement made at a committee hearing. He asserted, "I was wrong in 2001," and advised the committee to refrain from using "climate change" as it no longer accurately represented the issue. He recommended replacing it with "climate action."

In 2020, Frank and I reconnected through a small group hosted by Torund. At that time, we were a group aiming to define the language for the new economy we saw emerging and developing. We were at a crossroads, unsure of the right terminology.

The best part of the group was working with JJ Brown, a conservative who had worked for two decades as a prolific policy advisor to Senator Orrin G. Hatch. JJ drafted countless ideas into bills and ushered dozens of bills into law, including tax credits for hybrids and alt-fuel vehicle purchases and for alternative transportation fuels. These tax credits passed in the Energy Policy Act of 2005. He was also the staffer behind Senator Hatch's efforts to build a broad, bipartisan coalition behind the original tax credit for plug-in vehicles that passed in the Independence and Security Act of 2007. What I learned from JJ is that there are different reasons to support one action.

What I found so interesting is that JJ's principal motivation for promoting alternative fuels was energy security, yet he was able to partner with others whose main motivation was the environment. Building those types of collaborations was one secret to his success. However, he attributes most of his success to learning how to use language that brings all sides together. He said: "Without finding new language to talk about alternative fuels and electric vehicles (EVs), I would have never been able to get the conservative members of Congress behind these proposals and they wouldn't have been signed into law."

With his mastery of using language to motivate policymakers, JJ's contribution was invaluable. We had a good dialogue on how to craft language to bridge the various voices, but most importantly, JJ knew what not to say; he knows the language that divides rather than unites.

During the peak of the COVID-19 pandemic, our small group had lots of discussions on the various vantage points to circular economy and climate change within the United States. At that time, we felt "Sustainability" was too vague, and even though we were accustomed to mentioning "climate change," we still struggled discussing climate action. And the term Circular Economy still sounded new and foreign.

Through numerous Zoom meetings and discussions about language, society, and how to use our time at home productively, we decided to conduct a survey in the US on the sentiments on climate. We wanted to pinpoint how to talk about the climate and how we can foster meaningful conversations, seeking the perfect words to articulate the next steps. We conducted a survey with Frank on the "The Language of a Cleaner, Safer, Healthier Environment Survey.

Global Warming → Climate Change → Climate Action → ?

To our surprise, our study revealed that "climate change" had unexpectedly morphed into a "trigger word" that was instantly polarizing. The survey respondents showed us that just the use of that word is an obstacle for constructive dialogue. Yet, amidst this challenge, we did find hope that a significant majority (61 percent) now acknowledge the serious environmental threats facing America's future.

Climate

The game-changer involved moving away from the term "climate change" and start embracing the words "reuse, recycle, repurpose." Remarkably, ninety percent of the public already backs initiatives related to these three words without needing persuasion. They are prepared to support a policy or action plan if it promises a significant, measurable impact.

⊘**Reuse**
⊘**Recycle**
⊘**Repurpose**
⊘**Sustainable**

Words done right show promise, and what was interesting with the survey we conducted is that the one word we thought that had the least promise--"sustainable"--ended up resonating the most with the survey respondents. Torund was surprised and asked, "Frank, how can this be? We held a conference on framing sustainability here in Norway, and the results show 'sustainable' is the word respondents most identify with."

Frank stated simply that it is important to listen, engage in dialogue, and learn the meaning behind the words. He repeatedly reminded us, "It is not what you say, it is what people hear you say."

The crux is discerning what people actually hear. This is why we at RENAS invest in surveys and focus groups to ensure our messaging aligns with what our clients, government officials, and other stakeholders perceive.

When it comes to purchasing products, how do you typically label yourself? Consumer? Patron? Client? The truth is, the language we use matters, and it can shape our mindset around consumption and waste.

To truly embrace a circular economy, we need to start thinking of ourselves as users rather than consumers. As users, we adopt a sense of stewardship toward the products we buy, which changes our approach to the market and how we fulfill our needs.

By changing our mindset and embracing this new role, we can create greater awareness of the opportunities that exist within a circular economy. Instead of focusing on the negatives, we can demand that industries become more responsible and "conscious" of their long-term effects and actions. Ultimately, this is a matter of liability—for ourselves and for others, both locally and globally.

Creating a Closed-loop System: From Refillable to Recyclable Bottle System

> We see a world of **abundance**, not limits. In the midst of a great deal of talk about reducing the human ecological footprint, we offer a different vision. What if humans designed products and system that celebrate an abundance of human creativity, culture, and productivity?

--Michael Braungart, author of *Cradle to Cradle*

IN A CLOSED-LOOP RECYCLING SYSTEM the products to be recycled are kept apart from other products, or contaminants, throughout the whole recycling process. All the process parameters are known and controlled, keeping the materials at their highest level in every step ensuring high-quality raw material for a new product. In the right circumstances, establishing a closed-loop system can greatly benefit both value creation and environment.

As mentioned earlier, nature does not produce any waste, and I think it's safe to say that before the consumer revolution or era of mass consumption, human waste production was at an entirely different level than it is today. So, how can we identify closed-loop opportunities across industries and product ranges, and then design and implement them with triple-win results, where we minimize waste and create high-quality raw materials at the same time? We need a mindset shift about waste. As the saying goes, one person's waste is another's treasure.

My experience has shown that material recycling increases significantly when there is initial value in an end-of-life product (potential waste). Take, for instance, if my junk or wrecked car has some value to it that makes it worth my time and effort, I would definitely sell it to get cash instead of leaving it to rust and rot in the backyard or some random field creating a small pool of pollution (which would probably take its toll on my conscience and be an open wound in my guts every time I see it or think of it).

Similarly, in 2009, the U.S. Obama administration implemented the Car Allowance Rebate System (CARS), known as "cash for clunkers." This $3 billion U.S. federal scrappage program provided economic incentives for U.S. residents to purchase new, more fuel-efficient vehicles in exchange for their less efficient ones. The program's long-term impact has mixed reviews, but even with mixed reviews, it demonstrated that valuing "clunkers" could spur action.[74]

I've found that to transition to a closed-loop system we must change how we view waste and perceive its value. The preferred solution is to put the value in the end-of-life cycle as early as possible. One of the best examples I know of is the development of reusing and recycling soda bottles in Norway.

"The Norwegian beverage industry has been circular for over a hundred years," said Kjell Olav Maldum, CEO of Infinitum AS, the organization responsible for Norway's national bottle and can recycling scheme, in our interview. He explained, "In the old days, glass bottles were expensive, so people saw value in returning and reusing them. This was driven by cost. Back then, breweries had their own bottles, mostly local, making it simpler to implement a return system for individual producers."

Even though Norway has had a closed-loop beverage container system for over 100 years, there have been significant changes in the bottling industry during that time. The industry in both the US and Norway started with refillable bottles, such as when the milkman would deliver the milk and then pick up the bottles with the next delivery. Through time, this system has changed and is now mainly a single use disposable system, but the industry and regulators in Norway have still managed to maintain and even improve the efficiency of this closed-loop system.

> **A closed-loop system** is a type of recycling system where products are reused and recycled continuously, without entering the waste stream.

Framing of a bottle: Norway vs. US

Wealth is a leading factor in how the United States vs. Norway adopted disposable bottles. The difference between the two countries teaches us how we want to lay the foundation and groundwork to transition toward a circular economy.

After WWII, the US was the wealthiest country. A significant sign of wealth was the concept of disposables which quickly expanded to many products such as diapers, TV dinners, etc. We will focus on the bottles in this example. Due to widespread access to extra spending money, the U.S. enthusiastically adopted the concept of disposable bottles immediately after WWII.

Like we discussed earlier with President Hoover and the beginning of the consumer era, the road to the linear economy was more convenient, quicker, and promised immediate returns. This lifestyle provides great benefits that we cannot downplay, and that we all are recipients of even to this day. The regular Americans of the time were the first to own new cars, refrigerators, and everything else that goes along with the modern lifestyle.

With the rise of refrigerators and cars, the once-dominant milk delivery service providing milk on the doorstep every day became redundant, eliminating the daily necessity for the milkman's visit. Thus, a significant aspect of the US refillable system disappeared, and in its place came the disposable system. American economist Frank Ackerman stated that the idea of the refillable glass bottles "had to be unlearned in order to unleash the consumer society of the late twentieth century." [75]

The earliest survey from the Department of Agriculture on home milk delivery was in 1963 when nearly 29.7 percent of users had milk delivered. By 1975, the number had dropped to 6.9 percent of total sales, and by 2005, the most recent year for which figures are available, to just 0.4 percent. [76]

The refillable systems required cleaning and reusing bottles, which is an entirely different infrastructure compared to disposables. As we can see, once the switch was made, it wasn't easy to turn back. The shift toward disposable containers influenced the composition of the industry and society as a whole. The US has stayed on this completely linear system since post World War II, and it has no incentives to change.

> **Refillable bottles** are containers that can be used multiple times, designed to be cleaned and refilled with the same or similar products. **Disposable bottles** are intended for one-time use before being recycled or discarded.

Norway from refillable to disposal

Unlike the US, Norway was among the poorest countries in Europe post-WW2, until the discovery of oil in 1969 significantly changed its economy. The United States even aided Norway with the Marshall Plan to help with post-WWII reconstruction. As a result of poverty, resources were scarce and every material was cherished, with glass being highly valued. Soda bottles were treated with care, and Norwegians were conscientious about returning them. The mindset in Norway was that bottles = money.

There was high value in the bottles, and the sentiment was that the bottles were on loan from the producer, much like borrowing

a book from the library. In a sense, the user was borrowing the bottles to enjoy the contents (the beer or soft drink). This bottle return system was rooted in voluntary action. The end user was primarily motivated by a sense of duty rather than personal and direct benefits. Bottling companies added an extra charge for processing these bottles, but when consumers returned them to grocery stores, the grocer received a refund. The end user never directly saw this deposit exchange.

Formalizing the refillable system

In the sixties, the globalization of American culture, with its films, celebrities, and music gaining popularity in Norway, brought appealing products like disposable bottles and cans of Coca-Cola. This trend posed a challenge to the existing refillable volunteer system. The side effect of disposing of bottles and cans was increased pollution where cans and bottles were left in nature. Norwegians highly cherished their nature and were outraged by the growing pollution of bottles and cans to be found along trails and everywhere people went. The result was that the Norwegian government listened to the public and encouraged the bottle companies to partner with the government to phase out disposable bottles and cans.

While phasing out disposables, the second step they took was implementing a governmental-mandated bottle deposit system called The Product Control Act of 1975, which Minister of Finance Eivind Erichsen authored. He asked, "Do we have to choose between Environmental protection and Economic Growth?"

He believed economic mechanisms could go hand-in-hand with environmental protection and saw the government as a way to facilitate and advocate for business, people, and the environment. The deposit system set a price on the refilling process that benefited the producer

and the consumer. Norway saw an impressive return rate of ninety-nine percent of bottles returned after the law was enacted in 1975. It worked so well because the consumers and producers saw bottles and cans not as waste but as money. The incentives were clear and accessible.

The daily life of refillables

Unlike many kids worldwide who delivered newspapers to earn extra cash, we had a different approach – we collected and returned bottles. Growing up in the 1970's, I had the entrepreneurial opportunity of finding empty glass soda or beer bottles along the road, in the park, or by a hot dog stand, and even in trash cans, where teenagers had hung out the night before. It was my good fortune that these bottles had been left behind, because my friends and I would gather them and take them to the store in exchange for cash. This way we had money for candy and other little things we wanted. Four to five bottles would get us a Snickers bar or a new bottle of Coke. Heck, we weren't dumb – the bottles were money and not trash.

In Norway, the returning of bottles is not a class issue – everyone does it. Even Norwegian billionaire, Trygve Hegnar will return bottles. Not necessarily for the sake of the environment, "but because it is all about the money."

Again, words matter: Refillable vs. Recycle

The distinction of the meaning of words is crucial, and it's easy to lump everything under the word, 'recycle.'

Norway's system was fundamentally about refilling, not recycling. The aim was to keep the bottles in their original state and reuse them over and over. This was ensured by a thorough bottle-cleaning process. For a bottle to be returned, it needed to be in good condition; any broken or chipped bottles were not accepted.

On the other hand, the word "recycling" is defined as reintroducing materials back into the cycle, but they are not necessarily used again in the same way. While recycling of materials is done both mechanically and chemically, materials are physically transformed in order to be reintroduced into the manufacturing process. By contrast, refillable containers are cleaned and refilled and reused multiple times. This is why recycling is a solution for disposable systems.

Maintaining both the refillable and disposable systems can pose a challenge for bottle producers. The refillable system requires effort and investment to sustain, whereas the disposable approach often leads to added recycling.

From refillable to disposal system

Products change with the times, and in the 1990s plastic bottles arrived. Their light weight and durability (practically unbreakable) made them much more suitable for their purpose than glass. People remembered accidents where entire stacks of crates containing glass bottles fell over, spilling their contents and shattering glass everywhere; plastic bottles prevented such breakage but created new environmental challenges. Even though the refillable system was very successful it was important to find new ways. Outsiders often question why Norway abandoned the older refillable system, but ultimately it was less environmentally friendly.

- The challenge: disposable products were seen as worthless.
- The advantage: Norwegians were used to returning bottles.
- The solution: switch from glass to plastic, keeping the perception of value the same.

Environment Minister Thorbjørn Berntsen saw a solution by assigning responsibility to the producers. He implemented an environmental fee, incentivizing them to reduce waste and increase recycling. As the share of bottles and cans returned for recycling increased, this fee would decrease.

This approach motivated producers in the 1990s to establish an effective collection system.

It's hard to imagine today, but refillable and recyclable systems are entirely different, and running both simultaneously can be too difficult and costly. However, to maintain Norway's incentive for deposit bottles, it was decided to operate these two parallel systems together from the late 1990s until 2015, when the system became all disposable.

How does the disposable system work?

The government provides tax incentives to bottle companies. Let's say the bottle producer manufactures 100 million bottles, and ninety-five percent of them are returned. The company will pay zero taxes for those bottles. If the percentage is below ninety-five they pay a sliding scale tax where the lower the return, the higher the taxes. Also, this incentive ensures the production companies are doing their utmost to encourage consumers to return all types of bottles and cans via extensive communications and marketing campaigns.

$7.20

24 pack

The user is incentivized by being able to get their deposit back. When a user purchases a bottle of soda, they pay an extra 20 to 30 cents as a deposit, depending on size. This money is given back when the consumer returns the bottle to the store, giving a powerful incentive to not put in the trash, or elsewhere. This adds up; for a pack of 24 bottles, the deposit refund equals $7.20.[77]

Norway's disposable system is world-renowned, drawing leaders globally to study how it achieves a ninety-seven percent recycling rate for all plastic drink bottles. Ninety two percent are recycled to such a high standard that the materials are reused are for drink bottles.

Kjell Maldum, the CEO of Infinitum, Norway's version of the US redemption centers, states that some of the material has been recycled more than fifty times already. This means that fewer than one percent of plastic bottles end up in the environment.

Maldum says, "It is a system that puts the emphasis on the producer to pay for and devise a system that works. We think we have come up with the most efficient and environmentally friendly system anywhere in the world." [78]

So, what is Norway doing differently?

To put it simply, the nation has given recycling a value it didn't have before.

"There's an ingenious aspect of the Norwegian deposit regulation: it states that anyone who sells drinks must also be obligated to take them back. I think that's brilliant. It implies that everyone is on the chain of responsibility," state Maldum.

Byproduct of refillable = innovation

The refillable system in Norway resulted in the invention of the reverse vending machine (RVM) developed with SINTEF, one of Europe's largest independent research organizations in partnership with the firm TOMRA Systems ASA founded in 1972. "The RVM technology proved so effective that by the end of the year, the brothers' newly founded company, TOMRA, had installed 29 machines across Norway. By 1973, TOMRA was agreeing distribution deals across Europe and the US – and that was just the beginning of their incredible story of market and revenue growth."[79]

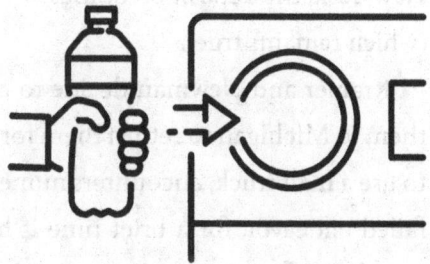

An RVM is just what it sounds like; it is similar to a regular vending machine but in reverse. Instead of putting in money to get a drink, you put in an empty bottle or can, and the machine gives you back money or a voucher. After emptying your bottle of soda, instead of throwing the bottle in the trash can, you can return it by using the RVM machine, get your money back, and, at the same time, help the environment.

The RVMs have enhanced the bottle return experience, offering a clean, efficient, and easily accessible solution inside stores. These systems accommodate both refillable and recyclable processes. With the streamlining of collection, TOMRA's RVMs have become a crucial component of recycling efforts globally.

Why are RVMs not in every American grocery store? [80]

Just because a great idea can work in one country does not mean it will be as successful in another. This was evident with the RVM and the reuse of bottles in the US.

The television series *Seinfeld* got into promoting bottle deposits with an episode that aired in May 1996 titled "The Bottle Deposit," where characters Newman and Kramer hatch a scheme to make money by exploiting the price difference in bottle deposits between New York and Michigan.[81] In New York, the deposit on bottles is 5 cents, while in Michigan, it's 10 cents (which remains true).

Kramer and Newman decide to collect bottles in New York and drive them to Michigan to return them for double the deposit value. Their plan, to use a mail truck, encounters numerous comedic obstacles. Despite their failed endeavor, for a brief time it humorously highlighted an uptick in recycling efforts.

Many believed that RVMs would be all the rage in the states, especially the inventors at TOMRA who oversaw the expansion of RVMs in Europe. Unfortunately, for all its success elsewhere, the RVM fell short of original expectations in America.

Why have RVMs not taken off across the US? [82]

- **First, a higher bottle value leads to greater incentives.** As we seen in *Seinfeld*, the high rates in Michigan caused interest in traveling to Michigan to get the return. In the United States the highest return rates are in Oregon and Michigan: 10 cents for depositing bottles and cans are considered the leaders in the United States.

- **Second, cultural differences.** [83] TOMRA believed that the RVM's capability to process all types of bottles would make it universally adaptable across various cultures. However, their expansion to the US market challenged this idea. While the Scandinavian culture had seamlessly integrated recycling with the RVM in Europe and some other countries, introducing the technology in New York presented a set of unique challenges. To successfully market the machine, TOMRA had to navigate the nuances of local politics and business culture.

- **Bridging cultural differences through cooperation.** [84] In Michigan, TOMRA encountered huge success, because it was able to find common ground with key players in the breweries, soft drink bottlers, the Michigan Soft Drink Association, and the Michigan Beer and Wine Wholesalers Association. Working closely with all of these groups, TOMRA was able to find an option that would work in Michigan. Like any good business, TOMRA discovered what was missing for Michigan to have a successful bottle redemption program and helped fill the gap. In this instance, it was not just to install the RVMs, but to create a fully automated depot, ensuring cost-effective handling of empty beverage containers throughout the state. TOMRA together with the bottlers designed an effective system ranging from grocery reception of containers using RVMs to backend material processing. TOMRA became a complete service provider, overseeing materials handling, accounting, and management for all types of beverage containers. Their holistic approach, which involved all relevant groups, resulted in a triumphant outcome for everyone involved.

"We are by nature a tech company, but to create market and opportunity we now invest in different parts of the value chain. We want to create new circular value chains and are willing to take on different roles and be the orchestrator to make that happen," stated Tove Andersen, CEO of TOMRA Systems ASA.

Today, TOMRA is the technology leader and has approximately 105,000 installations in over 100 markets worldwide. It achieved total revenues of about 12 billion NOK in 2022. TOMRA's geographic footprint covers all continents, and the solutions provided are increasingly relevant for serving sustainable societies.[85]

The key: the producers' responsibilities

While putting a value on the product is good, not all products can be deposited. The best products to incorporate into a closed-loop deposit system would be products composed of a single resource that are easily taken apart to return. We could possibly have a deposit system for batteries, LED screens, and refrigerators in the foreseeable future. The expansion of this kind of deposit system has not progressed, because these products are not a polluting problem. You rarely see a refrigerator discarded along the roadside. However, putting a value on the product and having a deposit system might be smart.

Extended Producer Responsibility (EPR) is defined by the OECD (Organization for Economic Co-operation and Development) as "an environmental policy approach where the producer's responsibility for a product is extended to the post-consumer stage of a product's lifecycle."[86] This approach is used extensively throughout Europe in the last two decades, and EPR solutions are now effectively in place for several different products like electrical and electronic equipment (EEE), batteries, packaging, tires, automobiles, zand others, and there is work in progress for several more.

Since 1999, on behalf of thousands of customers and producers, RENAS has collected over 1.4 million tons of waste electrical and electronic equipment (WEEE) from the Norwegian market, making sure that hazardous substances are removed and disposed of properly and that materials are being recycled using the best available technology. The collection system covers every part of Norway, even remote and little populated areas, making it easy for all consumers to find a collection point for their waste. There simply is no excuse for people to throw the e-waste products in the regular trash or dump them in some random place. From the collection point, the waste is transported to specialized treatment facilities where everything is monitored, traced, and documented until final treatment. This is done regardless of the profitability of the waste in question.

Depending on the type of product, the EPR solution won't necessarily aid in designing more circular products, but it certainly is a proven and very effective way to make sure products are collected, properly detoxified, and treated at their end-of-life stage. EPR is so effective that countries all over the world, on every continent, are implementing these schemes in their approach to combat their environmental challenges. Recent years have shown that certain materials are becoming scarcer and more critical, and EPR solutions can even be an effective way of making sure such critical materials are recovered and brought back into the economy.

Upcycling is the act of reusing discarded materials to create a product of higher quality or value than the original.

About WEEE Directive

The Waste Electrical and Electronic Equipment Directive (WEEE Directive) of the European Union was first implemented in February 2003 and focuses on reducing electronic waste. It requires manufacturers and consumers of electronic goods to recycle and dispose of these products responsibly. The directive aims to decrease environmental impact by promoting reuse, recycling, and other forms of recovery.

The Triple Win

"Teamwork makes the dream work."

– JOHN C. MAXWELL

TO MAKE LASTING CHANGE all sides need to win. This means, we need to answer the question, "What's in it for me?" for each of the following and ensure an appropriate "win" for each side:

1. The producer of the product
2. The users of the product
3. Society and the environment

I like to call this the "triple win."

The triple win explained

As I dug into the circular economy, I aimed to discern the roles of businesses and individuals and their impact on the environment. Each seemed distinct, yet as I explored further, their interconnectedness emerged, highlighting a triple win. The triple win is about allowing everyone involved in a process to win.

When individuals prioritize sustainable products, businesses respond. This growing consumer demand nudges businesses to adapt, resulting in a win for commerce. Their shift toward more eco-friendly operations directly contributes to a healthier environment.

Businesses are central in this dynamic. They not only react to sustainable preferences of the people but also influence them through marketing. By transitioning to environmentally friendly practices and products, they establish a symbiotic relationship between profitability and environmental conservation.

While businesses evolve to cater to the needs of people and the environment, governments act as catalysts. Through green policies and supportive measures, they can pave the way for the realization of this triple win. They can help align business activities with societal aspirations and environmental well-being.

Where does the government fit in? It is the advocate for all the parties and the glue that makes the triple win work. In some areas, government is not needed, but when we are working to change systems and adopt circular economy principles, the government regulators create frameworks that better society (or at least that is what they should be doing), making government the referee to help move things forward.

The purpose of the circular economy principles is to create a synergy of mutual benefit between people, businesses, society, and the environment. Recognizing this, we understand that our collective endeavors are steering us toward a brighter, more sustainable future.

The triple win should complement all business models, not compete with them.

In our quest to build a more sustainable world, several effective ideas have been introduced. All these ideas aim at one big goal: a healthy planet with thriving businesses. The underpinning of the triple win is that the one closest to the subject knows best. Norway's Minister of Environmental Affairs Thorbjørn Berntsen's philosophy was that the **business community is best at innovating, because they know their subjects. The responsibility of politicians is to set the direction. Politicians should not put their noses**

in where not needed. And I think that perhaps the biggest problem today is that we don't have this political approach.

Now, politicians are trying to create rules and regulations and describe in detail what to do and limit the possibilities within the business sector, but possibilities are needed to make effective solutions. In the bottle situation, the goal was clear: Figure out how to collect in a bottle or can in the most rational way.

Triple win and beyond

Achieving a triple win is beneficial for businesses, consumers, and the environment, with the government playing an important role as the facilitator. For the government, the guiding metric should be ensuring that businesses, people, and the environment all win.

Apple iPhone and the possible triple win

Consider the Apple iPhone: imagine if, through government-backed initiatives, customers could return their iPhones to any store and receive a $150 deposit, either in cash or as credit toward a new purchase. This flexibility means they aren't bound to Apple; they could even spend that money on daily essentials like groceries.

The intention of this incentive is to not be just another tax that goes into the big black public money pool, but rather an incentive for the greater good of environment and society.

For instance, an incentive program to promote circular principles would maximize the lifespan of products and materials. It would incentivize maintenance, repair, and upgrades, and enable a second life through easily available take back systems.

I believe an incentive deposit program would help accelerate the creative process in Apple (and other businesses with similar interests) to come up with a model that met the goals in the regulated incentive scheme. By using the creative force of the professional industry to innovate and achieve wins for all, customers would get better products and services, businesses would avoid extra taxes and get clear incentives to innovate and futureproof their business, and society would gain a healthier planet. This is smart business in my book.

From an environmental perspective, placing a monetary value on depositing phones discourages wasteful disposal. Jim Riley, the Interim President & CEO at National Waste & Recycling Association, emphasized the hazards of discarded phones in the waste bin, noting they often cause fires at recycling plants. With government involvement, implementing a system to add a deposit value to phones could incentivize consumers not to discard them. This would help prevent fires at recycling plants and ensure the return of valuable raw materials.

What I found when I dug into the triple win criteria was the ethos of Norway. There has been a long-held tradition of collaboration and finding a win for all. For instance, business associations work closely with labor associations and the government to find a solution that will benefit all. Sometimes the discussions get heated and end up in a strike, but overall, at the end of the day, there is a vision to ensure that all benefit or, when there is a downturn, that all take their share of the burden to lift society through the valley of dark times.

The reason this works well at the foundation level is trust. There is trust that a solution will be made in the interest of society.

I have found that the most effective wins are those. closest to the business or person. To succeed, the path to profit must be clear and uncomplicated. When systems become too complex, the incentive to participate diminishes.

This principle can be applied beyond just bottles or iPhones; consider the idea of depositing clothing. Imagine a system where you could deposit old clothing and receive a voucher for new attire. This would not only discourage fast fashion but also create a scenario in which everyone benefits.

The triple win collaboration: the industry cluster

> "Paradoxically, the enduring competitive advantages in a global economy lie increasingly in local things – knowledge, relationships, and motivation that distant rivals cannot match."

A great foundation to foster the triple win is to establish *industry clusters*. In the last decade, the Norwegian government and business community have embraced the *industry cluster* framework. It is one of the best methods to move more quickly toward a circular economy. The reason for its success is that that the framework is non-linear, non-hierarchal, and circular by nature with collaboration as the glue. The driving force is to find future sustainable solutions that would be uphill battles as solo ventures.

What exactly is an industry cluster?

An *industry cluster* is a collection of regional companies, technologies, and resources that relate to a particular industry, working together to produce similar and interrelated products.

Industry clusters were popularized by Michel E. Porter in his 1988 book, "On Competition." Porter stated that well-functioning clusters boost the competitiveness of national economies and have the potential to affect competition in three ways:

by increasing the productivity of the companies in the cluster

by driving innovation in the field

by stimulating new businesses in the field

About US industry clusters

In the US, clusters are funded by the U.S. Department of Commerce and administered by the Institute for Strategy and Competitiveness at Harvard Business School.

In general, each US cluster gathers together one or more primary industries with related industries that are part of its supply chain. US Cluster Mapping identifies 67 different clusters with between one and 62 industry members.

MIT conducted a study on clusters and concluded, "We see more innovation in strong clusters, and strong innovation clusters are also associated with stronger employment."

"The clusters have achieved a lot with relatively few resources. Knowing that companies that are part of business clusters have greater value creation and are more innovative than those businesses not part of clusters, this is a tool that should be focused on much more than it is today," states Trine Ellingsen, CEO of the Association for Innovation Companies in Norway (FIN).

About Norwegian industry clusters:

In Norway, the industry cluster framework was born in 2006 and the first clusters were called the NCE (Norwegian Centers of Excellence). It was initiated by The Norwegian Bondevik II government in the Parliamentary Report 25 (2004-2005) titled "On regional policy," which emphasized the important role of clusters will have in driving innovation-based business growth and boost competitiveness and innovation.[87]

This industry cluster framework is funded by the Norwegian Finance Department and administered by Innovation Norway, a state-owned company, and a national development bank.

Currently, there are 33 clusters, each uniquely adapted to fit Norwegian culture, slightly deviating from Porter's original vision.

Having observed the growth of the *industry cluster* in Norway and seen the impact, I believe that *industry clusters* will continue to grow in importance and have an integral role in the transition toward a circular society. What makes *industry clusters* unique is that they are centered around companies, and these companies are the driving force to develop innovations founded on the support of the government providing financial and strategic support.

Per Espen Stoknes, an economist and psychologist highlighted at this book's outset, finds that the challenge is being caught in a linear system where no one wants to make the first move. The *industry cluster* framework counters the linear society by making it more circular. It has proven to be an effective tool, because of the sheer number of businesses coming together. They create strength in numbers, providing trust and a safe place to innovate. Thus, working together in a group setting creates momentum and becomes the voice and power to break out of the linear system.

Industry clusters provide many advantages, including status and access to colleagues with specialized talents and skills. They also show valuable insights into how collaboration, networking, and a shared vision can drive innovation and competitiveness within a specific sector or region. The industry cluster is first and foremost endorsed by the government and then funded by the government with a third party administering the development of the clusters, the framework can be copied.

The most important lesson is that if you don't have the resources to join an official industry cluster, create your own. Seek out potential collaborators; there's powerful synergy when you work together.

Industry Cluster Successes

NCE Seafood Innovation Cluster: Based in Bergen, this cluster focuses on innovation in the aquaculture sector. It brings together industry, researchers, and educational institutions to strengthen sustainable growth in Norwegian seafood.

NCE Maritime CleanTech: Located in the Western part of Norway, this cluster works to promote eco-friendly solutions in the maritime industry. It has gained international recognition for its efforts to promote green shipping.

GCE NODE: Based in the Agder region, this cluster focuses on the oil, gas, and maritime industries. It works to drive innovation, especially in digitalization and sustainable technologies.

GCE Ocean Technology: This is another cluster focused on marine technology. With over 120 partners, it aims to enhance collaboration between the industry, research environments, and the public sector in the field.

NCE Raufoss: Centered around Raufoss, this cluster concentrates on lightweight materials and automated production. It has played a key role in strengthening expertise and capacity in the Norwegian manufacturing industry.

Eyde-Cluster foster international collaboration

A mature industry cluster founded in 2007, Eyde-Cluster started an initiative Battery Norway.

"We began working with the battery industry in 2016, and initially with material producers Elkem, Hydro, and Glencore Nikkelverk. In the summer of 2020, a series of battery cell initiatives emerged, and we reached out to Beyonder, Freyr, and Morrow to establish a foundation for industrial collaboration," stated Technology Director of Eyde-Cluster Lars Petter Maltby.[88]

Eye-Cluster via Battey Norway project has expanded the collaboration with formal alliances with other countries such as Germany, while also being engaged with the EU and other Scandinavian countries. Lars Petter sees the Scandinavian partnership has great possibilities of a powerful trio – Sweden, Finland and Norway can constitute a battery value chain in itself. He elaborates, "Finland has minerals and mines and can produce the basic raw materials. Sweden is good at industrial production, while we can provide the energy-intensive materials. Therefore, we must now be alert and be early with industrial solutions. The starting shot has been fired in the European battery industry, and we need to connect more closely with other European countries."

Common Goal

Government

Government works as a partner to regulate the clusters. Their goal is to maintain the common goal and prevent unethical practices amongst the companies and academics.

Businesses

Businesses are the core of the industry cluster. They have the supervision of the government & research assistance/guidance from the academics, but most importantly, collaboration amongst each other. With these three components they function much more efficiently that they would independently.

Academics

Academics including research institutions, universities and think tanks work with businesses to brainstorm the best possible solutions and work with government to ensure their regulation is practical.

Triple Win Today: One Water in Scottsdale Arizona

There is nothing new under the sun:
Water is water is water.
Or is it?

VICE MAYOR SOLANGE Whitehead of Scottsdale, Arizona, stressed in our interview that water is a constant cycle. Although it can be contaminated, the natural process of evaporation, condensation, and precipitation ensures its renewal. The water consumed by residents returns to the earth as rain and snow, replenishing the rivers and lakes from which we drink, thus continuing the cycle. Whitehead's passion for the concept of one water is to demonstrate to Scottsdale residents that treating and purifying water makes it drinkable again.

Scottsdale's Advanced Water Treatment Facility (AWT) is unique in Arizona. It purifies wastewater to drinking standards. While not used for drinking, it sets a precedent in water management. This model of recycling wastewater, now termed reclaimed water, is widely used in the region for various purposes, treated to A+ quality to ensure safety and environmental compatibility. Scottsdale's success has paved the way for new state guidelines, potentially allowing other cities to adopt similar water purification practices.[89] Comparing Scottsdale's advanced treated water with bottled water shows that the quality of the purified water is comparable to that of bottled water.

In the summer of 2023, *The New York Times* profiled the success of using ultra-purified recycled water, highlighting Scottsdale's world-leading Advanced Water Treatment Facility (AWT) and how the water is used by

Desert Monks Brewing Company in Gilbert, Arizona, to produce beer.[90]

Scottsdale City Council presented a challenge to brewery companies to use wastewater in their brewing process. Desert Monks has brewed two beers with Scottsdale's treated wastewater. The greatest challenge is getting people beyond the "ick factor" and wrapping their heads around drinking the treated wastewater.

"Right now, the treated wastewater is not part of our drinking water, but it can be," stated Whitehead and continues, "The key is to get residents to understand that wastewater treated with the world's best technology is drinkable."

Scottsdale has been working on various campaigns to convince residents that the treated water is clean and drinkable. The latest campaign is the One Water Brewing Showcase, a yearly event in November offering beer tasting brewed by the Scottsdale redeemable water. The goal is to show Scottsdale's residents that ultra-purified water is safe to drink. Whitehead believes that it will take a few more years for the community to fully embrace the idea that all water is essentially 'one water.'

Founded on the triple win: Scottsdale's Advanced Water Treatment facility (AWT)

Tourism is the bread and butter for Scottsdale, accounting for thirty-nine percent of the city's workforce, and one of the main attractions is golf, which presents a challenge in the desert climate where water is scarce due to its requirement for green, frequently watered courses.

In the late 80's, Scottsdale's Mayor was forward-leaning, and the City Council saw that the city was expanding by leaps and bounds, new infrastructure was needed, and it was not feasible to rely solely on groundwater. Other solutions were needed. In addition, twenty-three local golf courses strained the groundwater system by consuming about twenty million gallons of water in one hot summer day.[91]

**20 Million
Gallons
=
About 30
Olympic Size
Swimming Pools**

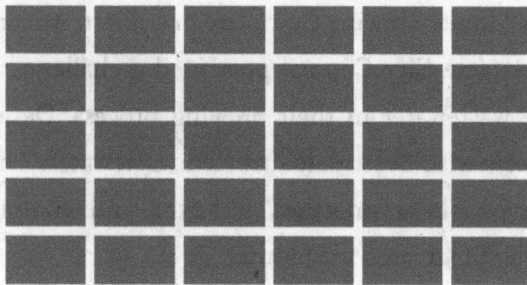

The solution was an advanced water treatment plant, designed to purify wastewater to drinking water standards for aquifer storage, complying with Arizona law. The vision was to implement a state-of-the-art facility that integrated all aspects of sustainable water management in one location, including water treatment, quality labs, reclamation processes, and advancements.

Whitehead stated, "To make this happen, the Scottsdale City Counsel knew this would be best solved by establishing a partnership with the golf courses that needed water. Golf courses bring in $300 million in business and tourism, and it was critical to partner with them so that everyone benefited." The golf courses met halfway and invested in "purple pipes" (colored to certify a standard for pipes carrying recycled water) to connect their golf course to renewable water. . Because of the partnership with the golf courses, Scottsdale City Council was ahead of its time and now operates a pioneering water treatment plant that turns sewage into purified water in under twelve hours. The Advanced Water Treatment Plant is internationally recognized for innovation. It supports the growth of northern Scottsdale and produces high-quality water used for aquifer recharge and irrigation of golf courses and sports fields.

The triple win here is that the government has established a foundation benefiting both the people and businesses, while ensuring water accessibility for all. This also promotes long-term thinking, a concept I refer to as "slow change," as I will elaborate in the next section.

The Power of Slow Change

"Plans are nothing, planning is everything."

– Eisenhower

I HAVE TALKED ABOUT change and how we can make small incremental changes that will have lasting impact. I am a fan of the design phase of developing new products and services. Prioritizing and being thoughtful in this period will change us from a linear society to a circular society. It takes time but will garner more benefits.

I like to recommend we take the path of slow change.

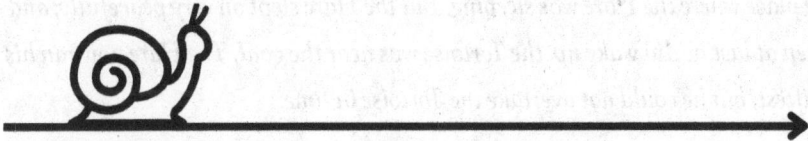

Slow change is making small, gradual adjustments over a long time instead of big, sudden shifts. It means taking our time to make improvements and carefully thinking things through to reach our long-term goals. This does require patience and learning as we go but will produce something sustainable.

Change is less of a battle when you take it slowly and in small increments. It requires flexibility and curiosity and, above all, foresight. There is an expression, "easy by the inch, but hard by the yard," meaning small movements are less painful than big movements. There may still be problems adapting to change, but being willing to move along incrementally can bring a smoother transition.

Slow change reminds me of Aesop's fable of the tortoise and the hare. The story goes like this:

Aesop's The Tortoise & the Hare

A Hare was making fun of the Tortoise one day for being so slow.

"Do you ever get anywhere?" he asked with a mocking laugh.

"Yes," replied the Tortoise, "and I get there sooner than you think. I'll run you a race and prove it."

The Hare was much amused at the idea of running a race with the Tortoise, but for the fun of the thing he agreed. So, the Fox, who had consented to act as judge, marked the distance and started the runners off.

The Hare was soon far out of sight, and to make the Tortoise feel very deeply how ridiculous it was for him to try a race with a Hare, he lay down beside the course to take a nap until the Tortoise should catch up.

The Tortoise meanwhile kept going slowly but steadily, and, after a time, passed the place where the Hare was sleeping. But the Hare slept on very peacefully; and when at last he did wake up, the Tortoise was near the goal. The Hare now ran his swiftest, but he could not overtake the Tortoise in time.

Research from Duke University shows that there is much more to this fable than a children's story. It taps into some fundamental truths found in nature.

In a study published in the journal *Scientific Reports* on August 27, 2018, Professor Adrian Bejan, the J.A. Jones Professor of Mechanical Engineering delved into the velocities of land, air, and aquatic animals.[92] He stated, "We see in animal life two starkly different lifestyles -- one with nearly steady feeding and daily sleep and another with short bursts of intermittent feeding interspersed with day-long siestas. Both of these patterns are the rhythms of living that Aesop taught." The research unveiled that some of the world's fastest animals, when considering their entire lifetimes, tend to be slower on average. [93]

What I found particularly intriguing is that research consistently shows that slow is smooth and superior to fast, even when we encounter exceptional cases that suggest otherwise.

Bejan extended this concept to the realm of aviation. He noted that, historically, the design of airplanes saw size and speed growing in tandem. However, modern jet fighters are a unique case. While they excel in brief bursts of speed, they spend a substantial portion of their service lives grounded. When their speed is averaged over their lifetime, jet fighters turn out to be slower than aircraft designed for transportation or reconnaissance.

These findings challenge the notion of exceptions and underscore the consistency of speed patterns across various species and aircraft. They emphasize the importance of considering lifetime averages when evaluating speed.

I would add that fast is better, when it is focused. For example, there are times when I drive on the west coast of Norway and need to catch a ferry to reach an appointment. The west coast of Norway is known to have the fjords and many small fishing towns still rely on the ferry for transportation. If I miss the ferry, I might have a long wait until the next one, and I will miss my appointment. So, being focused and fast so I can get to my appointment on time and hopefully make a profitable deal is worthwhile.

However, fast usually comes with distraction and less control over circumstances. When we drive over the speed limit and we rush to get to our destination, we may make a right turn only to find out we should have made a left turn – we backtrack hastily but have lost more time (and possibly missed the ferry and appointment anyway).

The universal saying that haste makes waste (which in Norwegian is 'hastverk er last verk') reminds us that rushing through a task or process will often lead to mistakes, inefficiencies, and ultimately the waste of more time and resources.

When reflecting on President Hoover and the second phase of the mass production era, I think we as humans took the fast road. It was tempting and new, with double lanes with fast returns. Our elders of that time probably asked, "Why not take the road with great short-term profits?" Human nature seems to have more in common with the hare to experience short-term gains rather than taking the slow, steady route of the tortoise. And yet, we should ask ourselves – did we take the wrong turn?

Was there a better and slower path?

Presidents Harding, Coolidge, Hoover, and leaders of that era saw the need to rehabilitate the public from the pain of recession after World War I. They frantically created processes to eliminate waste, streamline and standardize, and even put people on the balance sheet as consumers. Profits came with the public earning higher wages, more leisure, and a desire for more stuff. When things were purchased heavily on credit, eventually the banks could not handle the debt. In the short-term, banks failed, and this led to the 1929 stock market crash that destroyed Hoover's reputation as the president as well as diminishing Harding and Coolidge to mere footnotes to the legacy of President Roosevelt. Nearly everyone has forgotten Hoover's great contribution to the humanitarian efforts in saving Europe from starvation during and immediately after the war and bringing industries together to solve such problems as standardization of industry production, pollution from oil, and clean fishing waters. All well and good. But somewhere along the road, it all got fast, fast, and faster.

When I interviewed Reynir Indahl, Founding Partner of Summa Equity and a leader in sustainable investment and fund management, he stated that quarterly reporting and annual reporting place a burden on making short term profits.

If we look back in time, after the stock market crash, did we learn?

I would say we did not. We decided to stay in the fast lane and escalated even more into the linear economy, solidifying even more the lifestyle of make, buy, and throw away. Life got faster and faster, cementing our place as a full-fledged consumer society where the corporate culture set the pace of life.

It was not until 1934 that annual reporting for publicly traded corporations was required, marking the start of the escalation that tied corporate entities, investors, and the public to the seasons of the corporate linear timeline.

Progress has been at a break-neck speed in the last 100 years. We traveled down the shiny road with short-term benefits, and we must question if it was the right path to take. Mass production accelerated, driven by the demand for more timely information, particularly with the advent of quarterly reports.[94]

When I reflect on this, it appears that we've long been in an era of the Hare – fast and furious. However, it might be time to consider taking the slower, more deliberate route.

In the past, linear thinking prevailed among CEOs. Think of the days when Ford's famous assembly line was the norm, or when GM's CEO, Jack Welches, single-mindedly pursued growth and quarterly reports. Even American automobile executive and CEO Lee Iacocca focused on marketing consumer American pride. They were all about speed.

Later Steve Jobs adopted an autocratic leadership style, emphasizing the need to ensure his ideas were brought to fruition speedily. While Apple's organizational structure, with numerous specialist teams across the company, allowed for innovation, it also resulted in silos and secrecy.

Erik Solheim: a global environmental leader's insights from Asia to Norway

With his rich background as an environmental diplomat and current role as the President of the Belt and Road Green Development Initiative in Beijing, Erik Solheim sheds light on the sustainable strides of Norwegian company Jotun, illustrating the benefits of long-term strategic thinking.

During his visit to Jotun's Sandefjord headquarters, Solheim noted that its identity as a family-owned business is at the heart of Jotun's approach. This family structure has allowed Jotun to maneuver past the short-term pressures of the stock market and instead be able to focus on sustainable innovation and technological advancements, such as Jotun Green Steps, a program to minimize environmental impact across the value chain — from how they source materials and manufacture, to their methods of distribution, and their plans for reuse and recycling.

Drawing on his extensive experience in Asia, Solheim observed that family businesses in Indonesia and India similarly prioritize long-term stability. China's unique blend of private and state ownership still shares this common thread of valuing enduring progress over short-lived successes.

While Solheim acknowledges the stock market's importance in mobilizing funds, he warns that an excessive focus on immediate financial returns can sideline the extensive planning required for impactful changes, such as the transition from a linear economy to a circular one.

Jotun's vision for the ruture

Jotun's ambition for a broad impact is built on nurturing local relationships and embracing the decision-making freedom of its regional branches. Jotun GreenSteps, established in 2010, is our framework for improving the environmental footprint. Their 2030 vision is bold:

Achieve a seventy percent cut in carbon emissions. Ensure that renewables account for over forty percent of their energy use. Aim for a management team reflecting gender diversity. With zero tolerance for safety incidents, Jotun is not just dreaming of a more sustainable future; they are actively crafting it. Erik Solheim emphasizes that thinking ahead is more than good ethics — it's smart business for a sustainable future.

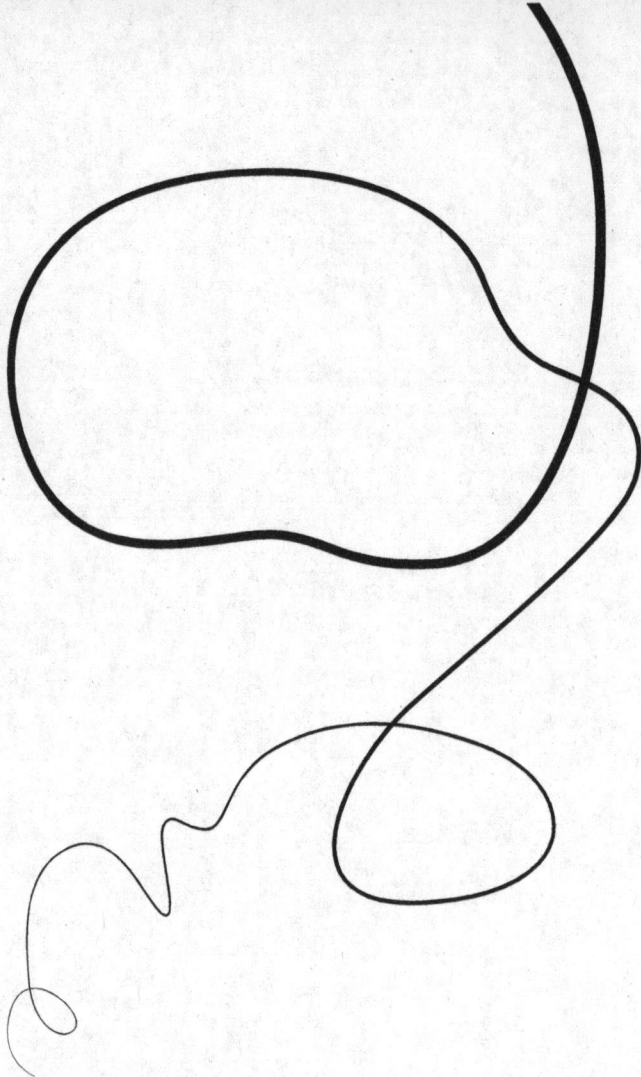

chapter five

igniting the momentum: finance and government in the push for sustainability

To change the system, we need government and finance to lead the way. The good news is that many initiatives are moving forward. This chapter will cover how this motion is becoming a movement.

We will highlight how financial systems and companies are helping us move toward a more sustainable world. There's good news: a lot of projects are already making headway. This chapter analyzes the progress, what is slowing us down, and how money and policies are working together to boost sustainability.

Navigating the Green Transition: on the Ground with Reynir

> "Sustainability is not just a buzzword. It's an imperative for business survival and growth."

- REYNIR INDAHL

REYNIR INDAHL, Founding Partner of Summa Equity, has been at the forefront of a monumental time in moving toward sustainable investment. He's been there as sustainability evolved from a sidelined consideration into the heart of investment decision-making. Initial skepticism from capital stakeholders questioned Reynir's heavy emphasis on sustainability and impact investing. But with robust backing from discerning investors and a growing awareness that companies addressing global imperatives are better poised for success, this sustainable approach has earned its rightful place in investment circles.

Reynir's guiding philosophy champions longevity in business. It's about elevating companies by focusing not merely on growth but on enhanced, sustainable solutions, leading to long-term growth. After a typical tenure of five to seven years, the appreciating value of firms under Summa Equity's stewardship attest to this doctrine's effectiveness.

What differentiates Reynir's approach is the deliberate intent to build companies for the long run by focusing not only on growth but on improved solutions. The resale value of these companies, after typically owning them for five to seven years, attests to the success of this philosophy.

Sortera success in sustainability

Sortera, a waste management service in Stockholm, Sweden, is the definitive example of how investment combined with a sustainable vision can lead to success. In the span of ownership, Sortera grew by more than sevenfold over five years[95] primarily by addressing the waste management needs in Stockholm's renovation market. The company's success can be attributed to:

Economic Efficiency: Strategic investments in advanced recycling facilities allowed Sortera to profit from the sale of recycled materials.

Holistic Waste Management: Innovative solutions were introduced to cater to a broader spectrum of waste, ensuring a sustainable approach.

Local Market Growth & Environment Efficiency: Growing the local market share and investing in low-emission vehicles minimized environmental footprints.

Moreover, the company began publishing annual sustainability reports beginning with 2017, highlighting their commitment and subsequently influencing their client base.

The importance of adapting to the green future

One key takeaway from Sortera's case is the need to look ahead. Reynir told me that companies should anticipate how industries and value chains might evolve in the next ten, fifteen, or even twenty years. "Looking at a quarterly report can't give you that kind of insight," Reynir continues, "Future-driven companies will be the ones that will achieve long-term success for all stakeholders—including shareholders."

Reynir reminds us that Sears, once the world's largest retailer, proved that any company could fail if it neglects the future and fails to adapt. The retail giant survived the stock market crash of 1929 and the subsequent Great Depression, and its sales were solid. In 1945, Sears reported $1 billion in sales, which would mean over $16 billion in today's economy. With all of this, the company that taught us how to shop fell victim to "the retail apocalypse." They had a minimal online presence and did not look ahead and adapt to changing consumer needs.

As the global market moves toward a net-zero economy, companies must revamp their business models to align with this new reality of circularity. The future is predictable, but only for those who are willing to adapt. As in nature, everything has to adapt to survive.

Looking ahead through the lens of sustainability

The real advantage lies in forming hypotheses about the future and actively seeking out companies that align with these projections. Reynir and his team's success with Sortera stems from this forward-thinking mindset. Companies that don't anticipate and adjust might face unforeseen costs, and potentially, extinction.

As Reynir aptly puts it, "To navigate the green transition, one must not only see into the future but start acting upon it immediately."

Profit in changing to the circular business model

> We who conduct business **must change the way we conduct business.**

--Unknown

We Norwegians take great pride in the recognition of Norsk Gjenvinning (NG Group) being selected as the subject of a Harvard Business Case Study.

This study highlights the success of implementing a circular business model. Through its recognition of NG Group's achievement, Harvard University has shone a spotlight on the company, acknowledging them as a frontrunner in sustainable waste management. The international community is also taking notice.

> "To navigate the green transition, one must not only see into the future but start acting upon it immediately."

NG Group was acquired by Reynir in 2018 through his investment company, Summa Equity. Annually, they process 2.5 million tons of waste for more than 40,000 customers and produce recycled raw materials, which are then used to produce new goods or energy. The collected waste is processed and sold as recycled raw materials to industries in Scandinavia, Europe, and Asia.[96]

I had the privilege of interviewing the current CEO of NG Group Bjørn Arve Ofstad who said he attributes this success to changing to a circular mindset, "Our statement or mission, back in 2012-2013, was recognizing that waste is much more than just waste. It's actually misplaced resources, and waste is a solution to the future resource problem."

I believe that what makes NG Group so groundbreaking is that they do not see waste as a low-margin product that belongs in a landfill. Instead, they have turned waste upside down by looking at it strategically as a potential value and implemented business structures to reflect their mindset. Reynir believes that by viewing waste as value there is a potential to double profits, while saving the planet."[97]

But moving from a linear economy to circular economy has not been easy. NG Group are working double time as they are juggling the traditional business model, which is their bread and butter, with the new model. The intention is that both models coexist until the disruptive innovative one gradually takes over more and more.

Ofstad elaborates, "Cultivating innovation is at the core of our strategy as we reshape our group's direction. We've established three core businesses: recycling and sustainable resources, green metals, and Urban Reuse. In addition, we're venturing into three new growth areas, which we term 'global solutions.' These areas focus on cable recycling, medical waste recycling, and plastic recycling. We're actively seeking partnerships with industry players who share our commitment to reducing carbon footprints in these sectors.

Furthermore, we're investing in technologies for bioenergy, biochar, and non-specific energy, aimed at producing energy with minimal CO_2 emissions. Our digital platform is central to this transformation, marking a shift from our traditional business model. We're dedicated to driving innovation and sustainability as we move forward."

And this is just the beginning. He continues, "What we have found out is that the value of a circular economic market in the future in Europe by 2040 is at €1.5 trillion euros. To get there, you need to invest something: around 230 billion euros in new processing technology and new facilities to essentially build the circular economic value chain. In addition, materials account for over a third of the CO_2 footprint in the world, so providing clear solutions, recycling materials, has a significant environmental impact. This is combined with the fact that it presents an exciting business opportunity."

What is slowing us down is government

"It is frustrating that politicians don't enact a landfill ban when there's a functioning market," states Ofstad. "A ban on landfills would provide a great incentive for businesses to innovate even more. The challenge is that government is often slow to respond. It is slowing down business."

Ofstad explains, "We, as business leaders, are also slow. It's partly because the regulatory framework doesn't provide the right incentives. Public procurements often come down to price, not

What is slowing us down is government.

sustainability. There's a lack of knowledge on how to evaluate companies on environmental performance. Leaders need to invest in sustainability and not be afraid of making mistakes. Good safety and health practices are profitable in the long run, and the same will happen with sustainability. But we need to change our mindset about investments and decision-making. We need better policies."

Better polices are coming

There's been a noticeable shift, one that even Reynir admits happened faster than he anticipated. The consciousness about global challenges and associated worries have grown. New regulations and the EU taxonomy have further pushed companies to be more transparent.

This consciousness has made fundraising for green ventures, such as his funds named Fond 2 and Fond 3, relatively easier, with massive interest from investors.

Unify the profit model with sustainability

What has been interesting to see in this last year is the proliferation of Integrated Annual Reports that combine standard annual reports with sustainability reports.

SINTEF, as we mentioned earlier, released their first Integrated Annual Report. CEO Alexandra states in the introduction of the report, "I am pleased that this year, for the first time, we are publishing SINTEF's annual report and sustainability report as a single, combined report. This is a logical step since research, innovation, sustainability, economics, and good corporate governance are closely intertwined. That is not just true in society in general, it is also true in SINTEF's strategy and day-to-day operations."

Value is no longer just the about the numbers, because what is becoming more and more evident and embraced by global financial companies is that what was once viewed as intangibles not fitting in an annual report are now recognized as pillars in the value creation of a company. I believe this is a great step forward for us to transition fully to circular economic principles.

> # Value is no longer just about the numbers

Bridgestone CEO Shuichi Ishibashi, who leads the world's largest tire and rubber company, stated about their Integrated Annual Report to Forbes Magazine, "As a global company, by responding to society's expectations and fulfilling our social responsibilities through business and social contribution activities, we hope to foster trust from society and our stakeholders and build foundations for further value creation."[98] Currently, integrated annual reporting has guidelines developed by The International Financial Reporting Standards Foundation that are used around the world, in seventy-five countries. The purpose is to advance communication about value creation, preservation, and erosion.[99]

Seeing companies take more initiative and responsibility in developing circular solutions gives me great optimism that we have ignited enough people to propel us toward a society founded on circularity and the appreciation of a nature-based mindset.

I think it is time that we start asking ourselves whether we are using the right measuring points, when short-term quarterly and annual reports dictate most of how we react and choose to invest and develop for new business and policy. Are these metrics suitable for creating long-term solutions?

I had the privilege of discussing this and other matters with circular economy specialist Vojtech Vosecky. He brought up some interesting reflections on a subject ripe and overdue for re-structuring: "about GDP and growth. We need to rediscover how we measure success, how we measure prosperity. How do we enjoy life without every little up and down of the GDP making headlines and disrupting the global markets?"

What is your answer to the question: how do you measure your success? What will you consider success for your family, friends, neighbors, business, and society?

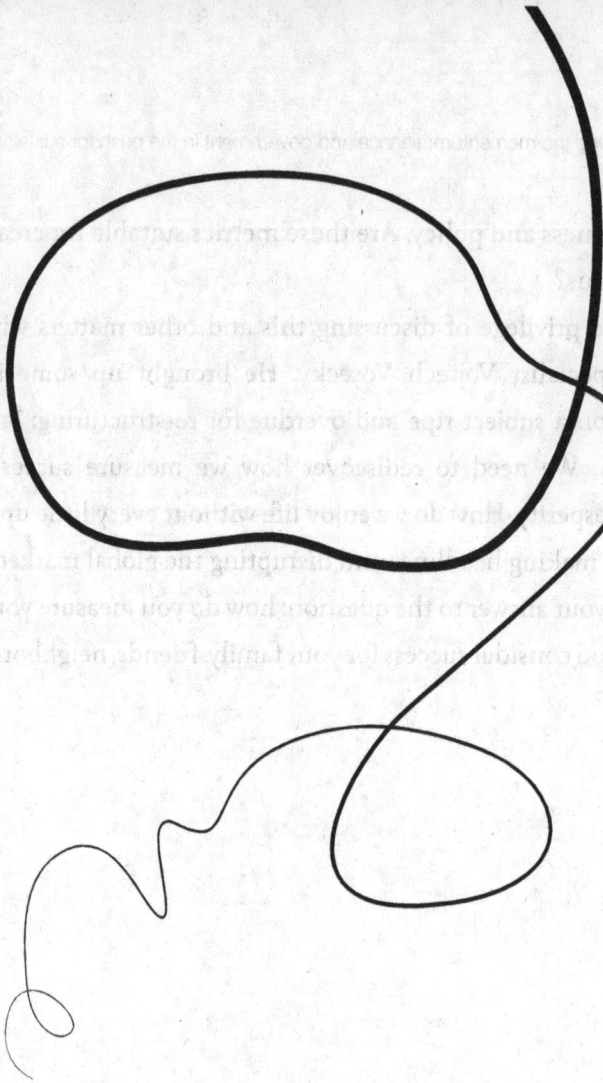

the acceleration of sustainability

*This chapter is about how we are moving forward into a sustainable
future faster than we think. We will highlight the ways in which
this is happening all around us, and discuss how to capitalize on
the momentum of the moment. We will also give the perspective
of the younger generation, who has grown up in the midst of the
acceleration.*

Circular Is Here

Q&A

> When we have arrived at
> the question, the answer is
> already near.

--Ralph Waldo Emerson

"CIRCULAR IS HERE." We were surprised when Ian Peterman, founder of Peterman Design Firm, said this in our interview with him. He then added that we are now escalating downward where transition from linear to circularity will go faster and faster.

I think we all suspected that this might be so, but it was something about having Ian's arguments confirm those suspicions that felt solid. I realized we were being too pessimistic and that we are in fact on the cusp of entering a new circular era.

Torund Bryhn, founder and executive director at the Nexus Council, brought up a book about the circular economy that had been published recently and said, "I knew the book was providing positive climate news, but personally, while reading it, I still feel like we are drowning and not making enough progress. Yet there seems to be a green pivot. Maybe we should be more optimistic?"

As a result of Ian's interview and taking time to look at our research with new eyes, I decided that the last section of this book should be to show how far we have come. I invited Ian to be a contributor. In the following chapter Ian provides his reflections.

Reflections by Ian Peterman on the Circular Economy and Sustainability

THE DAYS OF SUSTAINABILITY being a selling point and a differentiator have passed. Sustainability, especially when coming to products and their availability to consumers, started very slowly. The modern ideas that began in the 1970s, including the concepts of sustainability and environmentalism, started to be part of our culture through marketing. Selling "green" began in the 1980s as a marketing tool.

For the last forty years or so, eco-friendly, green, and similar terms used in branding and marketing as key differentiators have become commonplace and almost a basic expectation. While some companies really are trying to make a difference, many of them simply saw it as a marketing tool and a way to differentiate themselves as compassionate, innovative, or future aware. The marketing dollars spent on greenwashing, but not on truly sustainable and circular products, has left us at a plateau.

One result of green marketing has been to convince consumers that just purchasing a green product is all that's needed to keep our planet healthy. That marketing helped shift consumer preferences, but the transition to products that consumers actually want and that are truly sustainable is still in play. Now that the consumer has been sold, there is global demand like never before that continues to grow for sustainable products. It is becoming, and in many areas already is, an expectation that your brand is sustainable. It's now time to fill in those gaps of responsible consumerism, so customers can spend knowing their purchases are actually ensuring environmental sustainability.

On the coattails of large corporations using eco-friendly as a sales and marketing tool, the last decade has seen a huge growth in the number of sustainable brands in existence. Whether they use recycled materials or ocean plastics, offer repairability, reduce the amount of plastic/material/energy used to create the product, are designed consciously, are made for the circular economy, or in some other way create a positive impact environmentally, most of the companies coming out of the last decade are what I call sustainable first brands. Their brand story usually begins with a scene: they saw plastic on a beach in the Caribbean, a turtle with a plastic straw in its nose, birds caught in plastic can holders, or something similar. Then, they decided to launch a product that was more sustainable than other products. New cups, lids, straws, chairs, desks, you name it, there's still more coming out every day. And it's great, mostly.

The hard part is that many of these businesses fail to capture enough market share and profits to stay alive. Some are successful enough to inspire entrepreneurs to keep fighting the good fight, and their numbers show that sustainable products are the future and growing. However, the market has changed. I believe we have reached a tipping point. The slow pace of the 1970s is a thing of the past. Now, fifty years later, we're in the thick of the big changes we always wanted. Brands and products need new strategies to succeed in the fast-growing circular economy. The success of the circular economy depends on the success of the companies willing to support it.

Sustainable tipping point

As with every transition, new economy, or change in thinking, what got us here won't keep us going. Rarely is a founder the right person to take a company through an Initial Public Offering (IPO) -- let alone keep the business running and growing through its stable profitable part of life.

Sustainability has just had its IPO, and we need a change of guard so to speak to keep things moving forward without crashing.

Sustainability has just had its IPO.

The sustainability and environmental movement has spawned new ways of thinking. I believe that the circular economy is the next phase of sustainable global evolution. We're on that path now. Conscious Design is my approach to ensuring that we create products and brands that can live in this new economy and be profitable, successful, and beneficial to everyone involved.

To put this concept succinctly for our marketers:

sustainability is NOT a feature; it is an EXPECTATION.

What will keep us all moving forward is not selling sustainability, but just doing it in more accessible ways as needed to capture a global market. "Sustainability first" brands are struggling now, because using the concept as a marketing feature isn't adding enough value to the purchase. We will always buy a product because it fills an emotional need or solves a problem, likely giving us a positive emotion. We are emotional beings, and we've been scared and sold messages for 50 years now about how we need sustainability and to be eco-friendly or the world will burn. For the most part, people agree climate change is real, but a sustainable product just for the sake of being a sustainable product is an old trope consumers can see right through at this point.

We need products solving real problems that also happen to be sustainable. This kind of shared responsibility and win-win consumer exchange on a global scale will help achieve a circular economy in a more smooth and enjoyable way without the fear mongering and guilt tied into marketing manipulation.

> We need products solving real problems that also happen to be sustainable.

People care about the story of your brand and its founder, about how you're making an impact, but at the end of the day, this story should contribute to solving the deeper needs and problems your customers are facing. Your story and your brand are what makes you unique. As more brands come out with amazing sustainable products, they need to focus on their story and make sure the product has the right features and solves the right problems for their customers. Then, you get the added bonus of brand loyalty created when you and your customers can do sustainability together in a mutually enjoyable way, because if you can't, you won't last as long as you probably want to.

Branding for a circular economy

So, what does successful branding look like in a circular economy? Brands must continue to focus on telling their story. The brand and the people who make it up should be unique and impossible to replicate. You may have similar products to your "competitors" and everyone in the industry might be sustainable, but you can have a mission, values, and a story that are just yours. This is what people will find and align with and then enjoy buying your products. The key components of this storytelling done effectively will be accountability and inclusion. How can you continue to share your brand's commitment and the progress of your mission with your customers, helping them see and feel their part in solving the problems you both agree need solving?

Sustainability = efficiency

At its core, sustainability is efficiency. If you do it right, you can't be sustainable without being more efficient. Marketing has led consumers to accept or associate sustainability as something that just means a product is eco-friendly and not harmful to people or the environment. These half-truths are beyond their expiration date as time reminds us who's still in the game and who is not.

If you reduce materials and energy to produce a product, you not only make it more sustainable but more efficient. A system that kills itself is not efficient, nor is having unsustainable practices that drive us toward our own extinction. The Earth will last far beyond our existence; it doesn't need clean water to be a rock hurdling through space. Sustainability and efficiency are a requirement for us to survive as a species. Nature evolves to be as efficient as possible for survival, and the mutations that aren't efficient don't survive.

When I work with companies, either consulting or through my design firm, we don't push sustainability as a requirement. We focus on solving our clients' problems, (so they can solve their customers' problems), and we find the most sustainable and efficient way to do it. A lot of people get hung up on their idea of what "sustainable" is. They think it MUST be biodegradable, or it MUST be recyclable, or it MUST be repairable, or it MUST last forever! We don't know of any single definition of sustainability that fully supports every product or service. If we made cars out of material that biodegraded in a couple weeks, we'd have to buy a new one every couple of weeks. How would that be sustainable?

> If we made cars out of material that biodegraded in a couple weeks, we'd have to buy a new one every couple of weeks. How would that be sustainable?

Sustainable can be a vague descriptor, especially when you think about it through the lens of conscious design. You must look at the true impact of the product, both through its production and use, but also its end of life. Some products should last weeks or even days; others should last centuries. Toto create products that are truly sustainable, profitable, and create a positive impact, we have to look at so much more than just "can you compost it?"

Circular economy and sustainability on the global scale
The next phase of life for sustainability and embracing the circular economy will require not only local but international cooperation. The last example of global cooperation that compares to what's needed now was the creation and commercialization of the internet.

Even today, despite wars, trade disagreements, political coups, and other turmoil, we have kept the internet stable and shared for the most part. It took massive projects and standardization to create the internet as it is today. We have massive cables lying across sea floors to connect our continents, and while each country has differing levels of freedom to use, access, and connect to the internet, it's there and stable. Our global economy requires the internet to operate at this point. We are expanding that stability even further now with satellite constellations to provide even more internet coverage.

To keep sustainability going, and to continue its growth through its next phase of life, we need to look at how the internet was brought into existence. For 50 years, sustainability has been grassroots, convincing people that this is the right way to do things. Now that we are here, it's time to look at the entire planet as a system.

Circular economy is often talked about on a micro scale. This is great when things are grass roots, and we should continue to think positively about local-first initiatives and ensuring that our local communities are well supported. Progress requires us to also look globally. Few people acknowledge how much of a global economy we are. While I support local businesses and communities, it's important to point out that no community can exist without the rest of the world. The local artist you love to support could probably only create their art because of global trade. Before global trade, it was not easy to paint in every color we can now or to be able to get blocks of marble to carve, etc. Now, because of the global economy, I can sit in my little community and be a local artist, using the global supply chain to make it happen.

All the world's economies need a seat at the table to allow a circular economy to thrive. Not every country has the capacity or capability to recycle or deal with the waste from the products they use. Part of this can of course be corrected through better design and materials; however, consciously designing a global system that makes it so every country, down to the smallest ones, has access to recycling, repair, and other resources means that we can create circularity for everyone, not just everyone in a first world country.

Technology is quickly advancing and improving methods to recapture materials. More and more people are looking at ways to use recycled materials that currently are thrown away. For example, if a small country in South America could still purchase all the products they use now, but their plastic and electronics waste was valued and purchased by another country with recycling capabilities, this would help to boost the economies and lives of people in countries who don't have the internal infrastructure to handle the waste products they currently generate.

I believe that in order to create a truly circular economy, we must look globally and see the planet as one entire system. Pollution doesn't care about borders. Our solutions must also look at the world and make an impact across borders, which requires international cooperation at a scale we haven't executed as a species since the internet came online.

Rare Earth Elements Debate: One Obstacle on the Way to Circularity

WHILE WE ARE ACCELERATING on the circular highway, as indicated by Ian in the previous chapter, we are also experiencing roadblocks ahead that are causing us to pause, develop new policies, and encourage innovation of new technological products. The dilemma is that changing from a fossil-fueled to a renewable and more circular economy creates demands for critical raw materials that were not as important in a fossil-centric and linear society.

For example, consider the manufacturing of Electric Vehicles (EVs). Currently, on US roads there are around 2.5 million EVs. According to S&P Global Mobility, EVs could increase to forty percent of total passenger car sales by 2030. [100] In Norway, electric car sales in June 2023 accounted for over ninety percent of total new car sales.[101]

This progress toward EV adoption sounds great, yet the challenge is that the production of EV batteries requires critical materials such as lithium, cobalt, manganese, nickel, and graphite . To develop a battery requires an extensive global supply, spanning an average of 50,000 miles from mineral extraction to battery cell fabrication.[102] This includes sourcing lithium mainly from China, cobalt from the Democratic Republic of Congo, manganese from South Africa, nickel from places like Russia or Indonesia, and graphite, again, predominantly from China.

Though there might be a propensity to stick with fossil fuels, studies by the U.S. Environmental Protection Agency indicates that producing a standard electric vehicle (EV) might generate more carbon pollution than creating a gasoline-powered vehicle, primarily due to the extra energy needed for the EV's battery production. However, research has shown that when considering the entire lifespan of the vehicle — encompassing manufacture, charging, and operation — the overall greenhouse gas emissions of an EV typically remain below those of a gasoline vehicle.[103]

The third significant challenge is our dependency on other countries for critical rare earth elements. For example, China supplies close to 100 percent of the EU's heavy rare earth elements (REE), Turkey meets ninety-nine percent of the EU's boron needs, and South Africa accounts for seventy-one percent of the EU's platinum requirements and an even larger percentage of platinum group metals such as iridium, rhodium, and ruthenium.[104] Meanwhile, the Democratic Republic of the Congo provides seventy-five percent of the global cobalt supply.[105] According to the U.S. Geological Survey's National Mineral Information Center, the United States imports over eighty percent of its rare earth demand from foreign suppliers.[106]

These geo-political dynamics are further complicated by players who operate under varied rule sets, often dictating terms as they see fit. Notably, during the summer of 2023, we witnessed disruptions in the exports of germanium and gallium between the USA and China, when the Chinese government implemented new export controls resulting in exports plunging almost to zero.[107] This underscores the unreliability of depending solely on one country. For instance, countries like conflict ridden Ukraine supply indium, a vital material for production of touchscreens.

Governmental solutions

Nonetheless, a sign that we are accelerating toward a circular society is the determination of governmental bodies around the world to find solutions by domestically sourcing materials where possible. For example, the EU recently introduced its Critical Raw Materials Act.[108] In August 2023, the Biden-Harris administration announced the allocation of $30 million to build up the domestic supply chain for critical minerals[109]

Challenges with greenwashing and understanding the rare metal nuance

In the US, J.J. Brown points out that policymakers in Washington are focusing on rare metals and minerals, yet he states that in the pursuit of helping we can fall prey to greenwashing. He explains, "Right now in Congress (2023) there is a tax credit being proposed for the full domestic manufacture of rare earth magnets.[110]

The problem is that China controls a lot of the rare earth value chain, and we depend on rare earth magnets for EVs, large wind turbines, and major weapons systems, among a lot of other things. The idea of a rare earth magnet tax credit is a good one, because it's supporting companies who are willing to take on China's huge monopoly and try bringing rare earth magnet making back home.

There's a problem, though, with the way that bill is written. Not all rare earth magnets are the same, not by a long shot. The types of rare earth magnet you need to propel an EV, run a wind turbine, or make a weapon system usable differ.

Thus, some products are significantly more expensive to make and require a different mix of rare earths, some of which are very hard to get. In spite of that, the bill would offer the same benefit to the cheaper, simpler rare earth magnets as the more expensive, critically important ones. Unless that's fixed, it will be Congress that's greenwashed this time. They'll think they're buying US-made EVs, wind turbines, and defense systems, but instead they'll be giving a windfall to producers of the cheaper magnets in our cell phones and ear buds. Why would investors put money into an expensive, less-profitable rare earth magnet for an EV when they can make a windfall with a tax credit on easy-to-make, mass-market rare earth magnets?"

"The acceleration toward a circular economy has been slowed down a bit by the disillusionment that greenwashing has caused in people's minds. As consumers and congress get smarter and demand better results for their purchases and their policies, I think the public will sense that their core values and the products actually align. Once that synergy is established between what we truly want and what's actually available, the circular economy will really take off."

Again, we are faced with the challenge of definitions. There should be a classification of Rare Earth Magnet to ensure policymakers are not being accused of greenwashing when they are doing the best they can to create policy that works for the industry.

The other challenge is that there is no clear designation of critical raw materials that are across borders. It can vary by country or region, depending on local needs, technological developments, geopolitical issues, and economic shifts.

For instance, the European Commission periodically releases a list of critical raw materials for the EU, based on a detailed methodology that assesses the economic importance of each material against its supply risk. [111] In the United States, the Department of the Interior and the U.S. Geological Survey also identify critical minerals based on their importance to the U.S. economy and potential vulnerability to supply disruptions.[112]

While the specific materials listed can vary, the concept is consistent. Critical raw materials are those deemed essential to a country's or region's economy and which face potential supply risks.

> **REEs:** A group of 17 chemically similar metallic elements, including the 15 lanthanides, scandium, and yttrium, known for their unique magnetic, luminescent, and electrochemical properties. Used in various advanced technologies such as smartphones, electric vehicles, and wind turbines.
>
> **CRMs:** Materials of high economic importance and high supply risk due to geopolitical factors or limited geographic distribution. CRMs are essential in the production of modern technologies and green energy solutions.
>
> **Rare Earth Magnets:** Extremely strong permanent magnets made from alloys of rare earth elements. Primarily composed of neodymium, samarium, and other rare earth metals, they have superior magnetic properties compared to other magnet types and are commonly found in computer hard drives, headphones, and electric motors.

Let's innovate ourselves out of rare earth metal dependence

The changing landscape of innovative solutions is introducing fluctuations into future demand. Consider the changes in the composition of electric vehicle battery over the last eight years that have influenced the demand for specific materials. As technological breakthroughs continue, the market will likely witness more shifts before settling on a select few dominant materials and technologies. [113]

Dr. Cynthia Philips, founder of the 22nd Century by Design Fund, backs innovative solutions for social good. Her team secured initial seed capital for a US-based molten salt battery project by BioLargo, which doesn't use rare earth elements. BioLargo is known for its clean technology and engineering expertise.

As Dr. Phillips concludes, "There's a mentality out there that technology will dig us out of every challenge we face. While technology is certainly part of the equation, so are business models. But what truly drives change is people and communities, empowered by these technologies and models, demanding more from leaders, governments, NGOs, and even ourselves as citizens. This integrative approach, where everything and everyone works in tandem, that's what I see as the integrated revolution."

Vaping, the new fastest growing challenge

It is easy to hold onto a linear mindset.

One of the most concerning setbacks is our increasing dependence on inexpensive goods. We're heavily swayed by price, and this sometimes blinds us to wider implications: environmental disruptions, geopolitical rifts, and the concealed costs behind those budget-friendly tags. The emphasis on offering consumers cost-effective products often means valuing profits over long-term sustainability. Think about the surge of single-use vapes around the world: these are produced in vast quantities, only to be thrown away after one use, much like disposable cutlery but with the added complexity of metals. Unlike devices designed for refilling with nicotine e-liquids or pods, these vapes mostly have plastic bodies intended for a single-use after which they are thrown away. I would have thought that we would move away from creating disposable products like this. Companies should be accountable for the end-to-end impact of their products.

Vapes are a growing danger that damages our environment

In the United States, the CDC Foundation, a nonprofit supporting the U.S. Centers for Disease Control and Prevention, estimates that 11.9 million disposable e-cigarettes are bought by consumers each month.[114]

Unintended consequences of seemingly unrelated legislation

In 2020, to address concerns over flavored e-cigarettes' popularity among US teenagers, President Trump restricted certain flavored e-cigarettes.[115] This action unintentionally boosted the popularity of disposable vapes as an alternative. These devices soon gained traction in Europe due to their improved features. Major tobacco companies, such as Philip Morris International and British American Tobacco, have since launched their own versions.

Liam Humberstone of Totally Wicked, a prominent UK vape distributor, notes that while disposable vapes have mainstreamed vaping, there's been inadequate response to their environmental impact.[116]

More recently in 2022, the FDA has banned Juul, a leading manufacturer of replaceable pod style vapes, from selling their products in the US. This ban is currently on hold due to Juul's petition of their ruling (2023).[117] If the ban is upheld it will lead even more consumers to opt for the disposable versions. Even in states like California where flavored disposable vapes are banned, the underground market for them thrives with absolutely no regulation at all.[118]

The key takeaway: All of this is just to say that when governments are passing laws and guidelines that may not seem related to the environment, they should take a step back to evaluate the potential unintended consequences, environmental and other. Most issues are complex and solutions must be looked at from a holistic perspective, in this case inclusive of both public health and environmental concerns. Legislation, even when seemingly unrelated to the environment, should consider potential unintended environmental impacts. Complex issues require holistic solutions, balancing both public health and environmental considerations.

Our reliance on cheap, short-lived goods, driven mainly by price, often hides the larger picture: low cost products can come with significant environmental and societal tolls. A change in perspective is crucial, one that emphasizes companies' responsibility for the full lifecycle of their products, from production to disposal.

GEN-Z, the practical generation

I wanted to get a fresh perspective on the circular economy and Gen-Z, so I brought on Sage Toomey, a social media influencer and Junior Fellow at the Nexus Council. Sage gave us some excellent insights on the circular economy from her perspective as a member of Generation Z: "We are the practical generation. We do not fall for greenwashing." Sage said that her *green pivot* occurred when she was in elementary school attending a "green school" with the "Disney Friends for Change" initiative. This ignited her passion, leading her to become dedicated to environmental causes. She stayed passionately involved with environmental causes, even attending Greta Thunburg's school walk out protests.

> "We are the practical generation.
> We do not fall for green washing."

Disney Friends for Change

Disney Friends for Change was a TV and radio campaign by the Disney Channel in 2009-2011. This initiative involved using the stars of various Disney shows and movies such as Demi Lovato, Miley Cyrus and Bridget Mendler, to create songs, raise money, and do PSAs for environmentally friendly causes. Fans could go online and pledge to adopt environmentally friendly habits as well as vote on how Disney would spend one million dollars in donations. The campaign, obviously targeted at children, was incredibly positive and empowering. The messaging focused on how our collective small actions could make a big difference.[119]

Sage Toomey's Reflection on the Circular Economy

I **WOULD SAY** the most defining characteristic of my generation as a whole is apathy. It isn't always that obvious, because the loudest voices are the ones you hear and they can be very passionate sometimes. But I would assert that the average Gen-Z today is very apathetic when it comes to issues of the environment, along with most things.

It's important to point out that this isn't a denial that environmental challenges exist.

You would be hard-pressed to find a Gen Z-er who will tell you humans don't have a negative impact on the environment. It's more that environmental issues are almost never casually discussed in conversation, and we are skeptical about each measure: "Is it worth the time/energy/money/inconvenience?" So how did we get from the passion of the Greta Thunburg movement to this?

When the eco-friendly rhetoric was positive, it was easy to jump on board! As a child I can remember attending a "green school" and with that came pretty much only positive messaging. We were encouraged to take small steps to help where we could, such as turning the water off when you are brushing your teeth. Kids with parents of all different backgrounds and political affiliations attended this school, and nobody had a problem with it. The Disney Friends for Change campaign is another example of

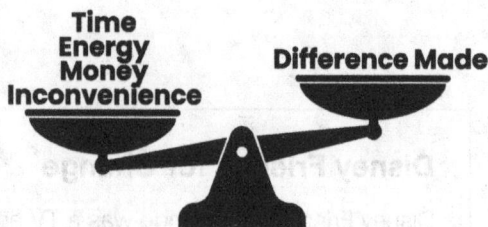

this positive messaging that was fed to us as kids, with lyrics like "Just one little action, the chain reaction will never stop." The world brainwashed the Gen-Z children to care for the Earth in the best way possible.

It's not hard to see how this generation funneled into movements like those spearheaded by Greta, but the apathy we have today crept in somewhere. This is because the rhetoric changed. We went from empowerment and positivity to shame and scare tactics. This started around the time I was in high school, possibly in relation to the high political tensions at the time (I graduated in 2018). Around this time the movement began losing Gen-Z supporters. Something that was once fun to be a part of became something angry and scary, so the less passionate supporters began to fall off. I mean, if we're all going to die anyway, why wouldn't I use a plastic straw?

Even though the shift in rhetoric had already started to cause the classic apathy you see today, the real nail in the coffin was the 2020 pandemic. Leaders had already been screaming that the world would "end" if we didn't do something extreme for the climate, but then something crazy happened. The world did "end" in 2020, and we overcame that. So, I think we're actually desensitized to the "end of the world" at this point.

This cultural apathy isn't to say that Gen-Z doesn't care at all. They just don't talk about it. There isn't much of a "movement" anymore. While I wish I could place all the blame on the negativity from our leaders, I don't believe this to be entirely the fault of the rhetoric. I think a big part of it is simple but true: people are just bored of talking about it. It's much more exciting to watch a debate about transgender people in sports than reverse vending machines. It seems that thought leaders in the environmental space respond to this disinterest by doubling down on the "end of the world" talk, but at this point the end of the world is old news too.

Despite the silence, the eco-friendly behavior is definitely still there. I believe it to be culturally subconscious. For example, no one thinks twice about secondhand items or reusable water bottles. We will always choose the eco-friendly route as long as it's convenient and affordable. For this, we can thank the adults of the 2000's who made a point to empower their children and suggest practical behaviors without all the shame and fear.

Gen-Z cares, but I think we have lost the *Cool Kids Care* attitude that drives the eco-friendly economy seen in millennials. This might be because the millennials still thought they were being rebellious, while Gen-Z was taught by their parents to care for the Earth. According to a survey, European Gen-Z consumers* are less likely than the average European of all ages to be "active greens." Such active greens are consumers who care about climate change, consider themselves environmentally conscious, and choose environmental sustainability over other purchase criteria. Instead, European Gen-Z members are more likely to be *convenient greens* (consumers who care about climate change but value convenience and price over environmental sustainability when shopping). [120]

With all of this being said, it's important for brands and thought leaders to consider that Gen-Z will not respond to ecofriendly products or initiatives unless they are:

1. Convenient/Affordable: Gen-Z will be less likely to go out of their way to choose products that are sustainable just because they are. They also have to be good and worth their cost.

2. Transparent: Gen-Z is skeptical by nature. Brands should consider this and be open about how exactly their products are ecofriendly.

3. Positive: I don't even think most Gen-Zer's have self-awareness of this aspect yet. But, of course, we respond better to marketing that says: "It's cool if you do this" vs "You are a bad person if you don't." Leaders of today need to return to the wisdom of our parents in the 2000s to draw us back in.

Gen Z responds to practicality

For example, my millennial cousin bought a product that I would not buy. She purchased six silicone bags for $27, and her argument was they were ecofriendly.

My questions:

☐ Is it worth my money?
☐ Will I actually use it?
☐ How many times do I have to use it to make it worthwhile?

Products I like are not just practical for the Earth, but practical for me:

Not just practical for the Earth, but practical for me:

Tesla: Tesla makes an amazing car, so amazing that they made electric cars cool! No one my age cares, or even cares to ask, if I bought my car for the environment, to save money on gas, or because it's an awesome car. Zero to Sixty in three seconds and no gas used are both great!

Dressd: Startup, founded by a Gen Z er. Rent out your clothes, make money, and save money by renting clothes. Benefits the consumer and reduces clothing waste.

Beyond Burgers: Beyond Meat is a plant based meat company. While plant based meat has been around in the grocery store longer than I've been alive, it is so much easier now to be vegetarian than ten years ago. This is partially thanks to brands like "Beyond" carrying their products in restaurants.

Thrifting: Many of my friends my age love shopping at thrift stores. They think it's fun! Even me and my sister, who do not shop for fun, always check the thrift stores or Facebook Marketplace first for random things we may need just because it's cheaper. There is no social stigma about shopping second hand.

Case Study: Myself

I used to attend protests and be very active in the fight for our environment. It's not that I stopped caring, but the passion was slowly replaced by apathy. Why wouldn't I care for the Earth? It's good! I love nature, and really love the animals who live there!

When I was a little girl, it felt like helping the Earth was something cool and positive to be a part of. The "movement" as it existed back then does not exist today. Now most eco-friendly groups are associated with anger and extremes and are not something I would like to be a part of.

Keeping this in mind, I still do what I can. For example, I drive an EV and keep the vegetarian diet I have my entire life. However, it is unlikely that I will give up single-use plastic in the form of to-go cups anytime soon. This is because of my dog, Gus. He loves to join me in the Starbucks drive-through every morning. Because of his presence, I am not able to go inside and bring my own reusable cup to be filled. Gus is one hundred pounds of pure crazy and could not be trusted inside of a coffee shop whether or not he is technically allowed inside. In this one situation, I have decided that the joy the drive-through and subsequent "pupachino" treat brings my dog is worth the single-use plastic usage in the form of iced coffee cups. Even though I wish there was a better option, that is just the way it is with where my priorities lie right now.

I will do what I can for our environment without sacrificing things that are important to me in my life. In other words, I'm always looking for practical solutions.

Research & Development Are Escalating -- Conversation with Alexandra Bech Gjørv, CEO of SINTEF

IN THE CURRENT INDUSTRY LANDSCAPE, research and development are essential for businesses to stay ahead and move toward a circular economy. As society advances, businesses are increasing their investment into R&D and innovation, because they are the lifeblood for keeping their doors open. In 2020, American businesses financed seventy-three percent of all U.S. R&D, marking a noticeable increase from 2010 when they performed sixty-nine percent of U.S. R&D and funded only sixty-one percent.[121] In Norway as well, businesses are increasing their investments in research as innovation is becoming more and more central to survival in the competitive landscape of the twenty-first century.

One of the greatest accelerations of R&D is within the field of circular economy. Ecological Informatics states that the concept of a circular economy has gained traction among governments, industry professionals, and scholars. To illustrate this growth, literature on the topic expanded from just twelve scientific articles in 2008 to a staggering 2,355 in 2020, marking an increase of almost two hundredfold in just over a decade.[122]

I had a conversation with Alexandra Bech Gjørv, CEO of SINTEF, one of Europe's largest independent research organizations, on the state of R&D and the circular economy. In tandem with the increase in scientific articles addressing the circular economy, SINTEF is experiencing higher demand for their research services.

"In the past, SINTEF often had to sell clients on their projects and initiatives. Now we almost experience the opposite. Now there's a high demand from the industry. Everyone wants to be circular, sustainable, and digital. And our job is to provide sound advice."

A shining example of SINTEF's influence is its ongoing collaboration with TOMRA. Tore Planke, one of the co-founders of TOMRA, worked at SINTEF during the daytime and after work hours joined forces with his brother, Petter Planke, to invent the Reverse Vending Machine.

As TOMRA expanded and sought further advancements in their technology, they collaborated closely with SINTEF. This partnership was instrumental in refining the Reverse Vending Machine, enhancing the intricate bottle recycling system, and pioneering the optical reading and deposit system. These advancements have been important in redefining the industry's standards.

The success of TOMRA is a testament to the power forging partnership with research institutions. Today, TOMRA is the market leader in its industries of collection and sorting products. Altogether TOMRA has approximately 105,000 installations in over 100 markets worldwide and had total revenues of about 12 billion NOK in 2022.[123]

TOMRA keeps expanding. It continues its collaboration with SINTEF and has also forged partnerships with other prominent institutions like CTR and Fraunhofer ILT, as well as universities such as RWTH, Aachen, and Brussels.[124] With over twenty percent of their staff dedicated to an in-house R&D department, investing eight percent of their revenue into R&D, and holding eighty patents, TOMRA remains committed to innovation and expansion.

SINTEF's vision is "Technology for a better society." They believe in generating value in collaboration with others including leading universities, companies, institutes, industry clusters, start-ups, and authorities. They develop projects that generate public financing for their customers, test and verification projects, and expertise evaluations for multinational research programs.

Alexandra states, "In the realm of the circular economy, collaboration is crucial. Drawing from our experiences, like with agricultural plastics, we know that multiple elements must align for success. This is where SINTEF shines—guiding collaborations, suggesting effective strategies, and ensuring stakeholders work harmoniously."

"In the realm of the circular economy, collaboration is crucial..."

and verification process and expertise evaluations for multinational research programs.

Alexandra stated: "In the realm of the circular economy, collaboration is crucial. Learning from our expedition, like with agricultural phases, we know that multiple elements must align for success. This is where SINTEF shines—guiding collaborations, suggesting effective strategies, and ensure stakeholders work harmoniously."

> "In the realm of the circular economy, collaboration is crucial."

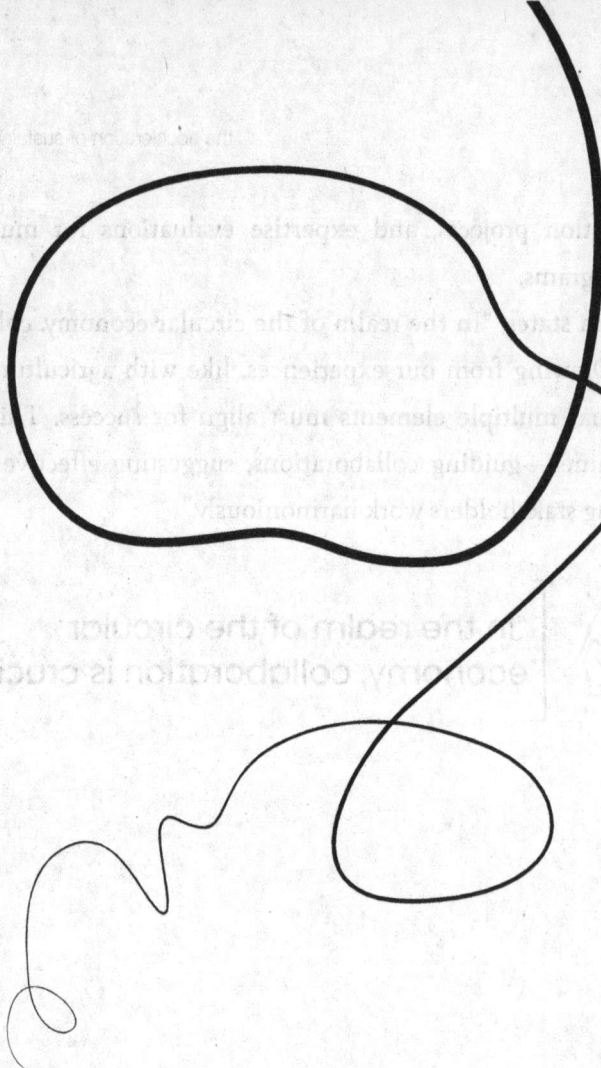

collaboration is the future

*Collaboration is the new currency and, in this chapter, we'll explore
how businesses working together are key to the move toward a
circular world. We'll also discover important lessons from real-world
examples and how to make collaboration work effectively.*

The Power of Collaboration

Collaboration is the new currency.

AS SOMEONE WHO HAS dedicated a career to environmental issues and the circular economy, it's discouraging to witness the vilification of certain industries, especially oil and gas. Too many voices seem to "cancel" these sectors rather than collaborating with them for a sustainable future.

Congress and collaboration

J.J. Brown experienced the power of collaboration when Senator Hatch first attempted to build a coalition in support of his tax credits for hybrid and alternative fuel vehicles. He explained, "I remember calling in the major environmental groups, alternative fuel groups, and vehicle manufacturers all into the senator's conference room. This was in about 2001, and it was pretty apparent that these groups had not been in the same room before. There was close to zero trust among them. The environmental groups were not too trustful of Senator Hatch's motives, they absolutely considered the auto makers to be their enemies, and while they promoted alternative fuels, they didn't love the idea of being in bed with the natural gas and methane industry folks. But the senator had already partnered with Senator Jeffords, who was a green, independent senator and Senator Rockefeller who was a strong Democrat. Each of the groups was in there, because there was at least one senator they trusted, and they trusted that that one senator would protect their interests. The Wall Street Journal even did an article about the collaboration stating that it was the first time the auto alliance and the environmental groups had worked together on legislation."

"It took a lot of work for me to keep all these groups together as we figured out what technologies would actually benefit the environment and would really make a difference. I left it up to the environmental groups to determine the benchmarks for environmental benefits, and by doing that, they began to trust that Senator Hatch was committed to substantial results. One environmental group dropped out, because they didn't want to be associated with the automakers, and a few automakers dropped out when they realized we wouldn't reward them for technologies that didn't produce the results the environmentalists wanted to see. It was a pretty big moment when Hatch held firm on the standards the environmental groups set up, even though we lost some automakers in the process. The mood really changed, and things felt safe and collaborative from that point on."

"In the end we came up with a major legislative proposal that had strong support from all three sectors, the alternative fuel groups, the automakers, and environmentalists. It took a couple of Congresses to get it enacted into law, but it may surprise some folks to hear that it was actually President George W. Bush who got it done for us. We had failed to get it done under President Clinton, and when Bush came into the White House, he made it his top priority to pass a major energy bill. Thanks to Senator Hatch's relationship with Bush, we were able to get into the White House very early on with our diverse group of interests. His top energy person didn't even have his desk delivered yet when we met with him. I sold him hard on the energy security benefits of our proposal, and the environmentalists, who, I might add, didn't feel all that comfortable being there, made the case for the environmental benefits. He was as impressed with our coalition as he was with the proposal, and he put our proposal, basically word for word, into the President's Energy Blueprint, which helped it get enacted as part of the Energy Policy Act of 2005."

The lesson J.J. shared with me emphasized the importance of listening and crafting a bill with multiple incentives rather than offering a one-size-fits-all solution. By designing a bill that addresses energy security, climate change, and the energy industry simultaneously, success becomes more likely. Crucially, the title of the bill needs to be neutral. This ensures that all parties can confidently present it to their supporters. If the bill had "climate change" in its title, those championing it solely for energy security would not have backed it. Therefore, the approach should be to first identify the mutual benefits; second, ensure each party perceives enough of a win to support the bill; then lastly, craft a pitch that's neutral enough to appeal to all involved parties.

The journey to unify around energy

Leif Johan Sevland, the President and CEO of ONS, has been a champion of integration and collaboration. Since joining the ONS board in 2008, he recognized the promising relationship between the oil, gas, and renewables sectors. "We started focusing on trust-building between different energy sectors back in 2008," he reflects. "Oil and gas lean on renewables to shrink carbon footprints and embrace innovative technologies. In turn, the renewables draw upon the capital and organizational strengths of the seasoned oil and gas sectors."

Leif Johan's reflections on ONS 2018 encapsulate the trajectory of this collaborative spirit. "The transition has been almost seamless," he muses, "2018 marked a watershed moment. The ONS 2018 opening ceremony signaled acceptance from traditional oil aficionados, integrating diverse industry segments and unlocking their combined potential."

Over the years, Leif Johan has spearheaded efforts to cultivate these collaborations, emphasizing mutual growth.

Building this mutual relationship was by no means an easy task. It

demanded actions that went
beyond typical boardroom
discussions. Whether
through intimate breakfast
gatherings or broad-scale
conventions, the aim was
to nurture a genuine spirit
of collaboration. The oil
industry made it clear: they are not merely using window dressing to look
green. They are working on becoming more sustainable

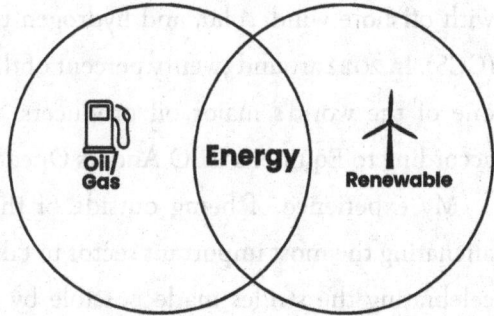

Central to this evolution was adopting a unified approach. By bringing
together representatives from various sectors, conversations shifted from
individual narratives to collective dialogues. These gatherings became
hubs of innovation, collective brainstorming, and shared growth. Field
trips and roundtable discussions were the arenas where diverse ideas came
together to form actionable strategies.

But the spirit of unity wasn't limited to these meetings. It was also
evident in the sector's evolving language. Instead of distinguishing
between "renewable" and "oil and gas," the industry leaned into the
broader term "energy." This subtle change in terminology highlighted a
deeper transformation, emphasizing shared objectives over the differences
between sectors.

The journey, though challenging, was not a solitary one. Many players
stepped onto the field, each bringing their unique strengths. But if one
were to spotlight a figure who stood at the crossroads of this change, it
would be Leif Johan and his organization. Their crucial role ensured that
the energy sector's collaborative approach wasn't just a vision but a great
success.

Today, the conference does not differentiate between renewables and
oil/gas as these fossil fuel companies now have integrated their portfolios

with offshore wind, solar, and hydrogen to Carbon Capture and Storage (CCS). In 2022 around twenty percent of the gross investments of Equinor, one of the world's major oil producers, will be in renewable energy, s according to Equinor's CEO Anders Opedal.[125]

My experience of being outside of the energy sector is that we are alienating the most important sector to take us to a circular society. While celebrating the strides made possible by oil, such as everyday products ranging from our shoes to our laptops, we're now beginning to collectively steer toward sustainable futures. The pressing need to transition from non-renewable resources has never been more apparent.

At RENAS AS, we identified the potential of ONS as a force for change and decided to partner with them. The shared objective was to spotlight circular principles at the 2022 conference. This move wasn't merely self-promotion; it aimed to enrich dialogue on the circular economy. The outpouring of positive feedback and our booth's nomination among the top seven stands underscored the industry's yearning for novel, cooperative solutions.

If our ambition is to transition away from fossil-based energy systems, our strategy should hinge on engaging the energy industry, not alienating them. Such conversations shouldn't be initiated with criticism but with collaboration. Let's recognize the indispensable role these industries have played in shaping our lives and join hands with them to chart a more sustainable trajectory.

Our alliance with ONS reaffirms the essence of collaboration. Together, we're channeling efforts to re-envision a sustainable, forward-looking energy landscape. In the spirit of collaboration, we partnered on the 2022 ONS – RENAS Circular Economy Study to assess how participants of the ONS conference viewed the adoption of circular principles. I was surprised to learn, but Jon Are Rørtveit, the VP of ONS, was not, that nine out of ten attendees were ready to transition to a circular economy. This resounding approval marks an encouraging change in the energy industry's mindset, a clear commitment to putting action behind words. It was noteworthy that seventy percent of the survey respondents were from energy companies, with a significant eighty percent of them in leadership roles.

And half of the respondents expressed the view that this transition is progressing too slowly. Even the energy sector wants the transition now.

Driving force for change-Skift: Business Climate Leaders [126]

"Creating a better world requires teamwork, partnerships, and collaboration, as we need an entire army of companies to work together to build a better world within the next few decades. This means corporations must embrace the benefits of cooperating with one another."

--Simon Mainwaring

One organization that I am very proud to have been part of since its founding in 2019 is Skift: Business Climate Leaders. Skift resembles industry clusters in its belief in collaboration, but it is a network that consists of over sixty companies--including both some of the largest companies in Norway and small companies--with the mission to work together to galvanize the business sector to take the lead and demonstrate the business opportunities presented by the green transition. The goal is to work toward this transition through collaboration, networking, competence development, and political influence to promote three broad overarching measures:

First, polluting must become more expensive. We need to count emissions as we count money.

Second, we must impose stricter requirements for green purchases, by demanding ambitious environmental, climate, and sustainability criteria in procurement.

Third, we must set higher standards for climate reporting and budgeting in Norwegian companies.

The Skift network was started in 2015 by three likeminded friends: Jens Ulltveit-Moe, a prominent Norwegian business owner known for his influence in the shipping, energy, and investment sectors and his passion for the environment; Frank Jaegtnes, the CEO of Electro Association, and; Nina Jensen, head of the WWF Norway. Together they formed an informal business network that they called Norway 20-30-40. The reason for the name was to communicate its goal: national climate commitments to reducing climate emissions by forty percent by 2030.

Frank stated, "The vision was for industry leaders from various sectors to utilize their competitiveness and together, as a force, have inspiration of the collective to have the courage to innovate within their companies. By uniting on key messages, the collective strength of numerous businesses would instill trust, ensuring politicians believe in and act upon the united message."

Frank continues, "By coming together, we are stronger and create trust. It's through unity in numbers that we foster trust in making transformative changes. Together, we break the system and inspire belief in the new direction."

The 20-30-40 group kept growing, and in 2019 it was decided to get help from Bjørn Kjærand Haugland, who helped co-found Skift: Business Climate Leaders, as the CEO.

Today, Skift boasts more than sixty dedicated members.

Bjørn Haugland explains, "We represent businesses across various sectors, giving us a powerful voice. We can highlight effective solutions and regulations that will enhance our competitiveness in Europe and beyond. When someone from construction collaborates closely with someone in transportation or food production, there's much we can learn from each other." He concludes, "It's all about learning from others and making the best choices for one's company."

"We may be a small country, but we possess a society with a high degree of trust. We have abundant resources, not just financial, but more importantly, human resources. We can make decisions swiftly, positioning ourselves as a showcase that other nations aspire to learn from.

Together we are stronger, and I have observed over the years how Skift has been influential in moving the political agenda, aiding businesses in fulfilling their role in transitioning to a circular economy.

In Skift, the vision is to transform Norway into a laboratory for solutions not just needed by Norway, but also by the world."

First, look at ourselves

Bjørn states, "What we value highly in Skift is that we prioritize looking at ourselves first."

I agree. The most important thing we can do is to evaluate how we can utilize who we are and what we have, and what we do, while at the same time draw inspiration from others and share abundantly. That is Skift's primary approach: look at the person in the mirror first.

One of the requirements of being a member of Skift is that the CEO has to be directly involved in the vision and work of Skift. Skift upholds its principles and has even requested key organizations to depart if they cannot align with its vision and mission. This unwavering commitment to its principles has cultivated trust and respect among the members, establishing Skift as a doer, an organization of action.

One notable company that stands out in this regard is Ruter, the public transport authority for Oslo and Akershus counties in Norway. I had the privilege of interviewing Ruter's CEO and its Managing Director. CEO Bernt Reitan Jenssen explained, "We generate around 11 billion NOKs in revenue and have approximately 400 million trips per year. This translates to around 1.2 million trips per day, which makes up about fifty-five percent of all trips in Norway."

What makes Skift unique is that there's no proxy; CEOs must be directly engaged. Bernt has been an active member and signed the 10 principles developed by Skift. The first principle is to be engaged, and the second is to find and develop new business models. Bernt has been leading the way in showing how to use the governmental procurement process to ensure transition to the circular economy.

Procurement constitutes a significant portion of Ruter's total budget. Out of a budget of around 10 billion NOKs, purchases account for about 8 billion kroner. The variations among different types of procurements and contract types are vast, with operators for buses, trams, metros, boats and more. In general, public procurement accounts for sixteen percent of the total climate footprint in Norway

For instance, through procurement Ruter seeks vendors and suppliers that can provide solutions for "zero or low emissions and circularity, and endeavor to avoid using chemicals that are hazardous to human health and the environment, particularly in the priority categories: transport, construction, building and property, food and catering services, plastic products and products containing plastics, ICT/electrical and electronic equipment, batteries, furniture, and textiles."[127]

"The Norwegian government takes the position that public procurement is a key policy instrument for achieving the transition to circular economy to meet its climate and environment targets."[128]

"What this means is that through procurements the government will be able to influence market developments in a desirable direction, which will contribute to Norway achieving important goals for society while strengthening competitiveness in Norwegian business and industry. The vision is that, instead of government lagging behind and being an obstacle to the transition to circular economy, the "public sector may, through increased use of innovative procurement, become a stronger driver for innovation in society. Innovative procurement has a positive impact on the public sector as a contracting authority, on business and industry as suppliers, as well as on the general population."[129]

"And I think we'd be in trouble if we lost our curiosity. It's what allows us to find new solutions and devote time to understanding problems. Those who are curious will never give up seeking a solution," Bernt concludes.

> "And I think we'd be in trouble if we lost our curiosity. It's what allows us to find new solutions and devote time to understanding problems. Those who are curious will never give up seeking a solution"

Right Strategy and Teamwork make the dream work

When I think of collaboration and industry clusters' impact, I am reminded of American football, particularly the San Francisco 49ers from the early 1980s to the mid-90s.

Why?

Well, to me, the San Francisco 49ers demonstrated the power of a strong vision, the power of a leader to instill a culture, and the power of a few who responded to the call and ignited the rest of the team. These qualities solidified the San Francisco 49ers to be the only football team to make the Super Bowl five times and win all five in fifteen years.

In the 1980s as a teenager living in Menlo Park, California, I was proud to call the San Francisco 49ers my home team. It was an exciting period to be a 49ers fan, watching with anticipation as wide receiver Jerry Rice caught passes from quarterback Joe Montana. Together, they led the team to back-to-back Super Bowl victories in 1989 and 1990. Their synergy electrified the world of American football.

When we investigate a bit further, the creation of the winning team started in the early 80s with Head Coach Billy Walsh guiding the way to developing a winning team culture. Coach Walsh discovered Joe Montana and Jerry Rice and helped them train to be their best and inspire others to be their best. From 1981 to 1995, the 49ers reached the Super Bowl five times and won all five, setting a record yet to be beaten.

What's intriguing is that Coach Walsh contributed two Super Bowl wins, Joe Montana contributed three, and Jerry Rice two, each overlapping each other and building upon the other's contribution. Together they created a legacy of five Super Bowl victories for the 49ers.

What does this have to do with Industry Clusters and collaboration?

True collaboration starts with the spark of an individual who inspires others to create a vision grander themselves. If the vision is grand enough, it becomes the light that attracts others to it. A vision spans layers of time and generations, like the 49ers many years of winning the Super Bowl. Coach Walsh did not just build a vision; he built a legacy.

Some are like Coach Walsh, setting the framework. Others are like Joe Montana, leading the team with precision, while some, like Jerry Rice, shine brilliantly when the moment comes. In between are the offensive and defensive team players, the water boy, the equipment managers, the trainers, the assistant coaches— all contributing and doing their part.

> Moving toward a circular economy with small steps will ultimately make the winning pass, the winning touchdown, and winning the game. And it all comes down to each of us taking our role seriously, knowing that our actions matter.

Collaboration with impact is legacy building; in such circumstances, the founder rarely gets to be part of the greatest win. Coach Walsh retired before the two back-back Super Bowl wins in 1989 and 1990. Winning collaboration spans over time and is a team sport where everyone has a role that overlaps roles and time. Can you imagine what we could do if we all exhibited the same level of collaboration toward creating true sustainability with circular economy principles?

Bringing circularity, equity, & design together for the future

We must be practical, but we should do it beautifully. Today, the circular economy is here, even if in its infancy. To bring it over the edge and into the collective consciousness, we must not only build upon the practical lessons we've learned and keep our solutions practical, we must bring beauty and ease to it, just as Apple did for the smart phone. In creating a collective shift that people are excited about, it must be enjoyable, beautiful, and get the job done.

Conscious DesignHaus, founded by Ian Peterman, is doing just that by bringing forward the timeless concepts of the Bauhaus movement in order to bring sexy to circularity and make circularity attractive to the masses, so that being circular is seen as fashionable, classy, and easy.

The thesis behind Conscious DesignHaus is in 3 parts. First, that every person is a polymath, a wealth of inner connections of areas of study, experiences, and ideas, that become available for any design solution. Second, that everyone, including the designer, is a problem solver. And third, that there is no difference between a "creative" person and a "non-creative" person; this is simply another silo we have created on ourselves.

The goal of Conscious DesignHaus is not only to help designers as we think of them today, but to influence and impact children and communities through local programs helping to create a society in which repair, recycling, and reuse create products that are cool and interesting. Quick change requires helping people at every stage of life to make changes and see what they can do and what others have done. We learn by copying others and have for thousands of years. Conscious DesignHaus will exist physically in cultural hubs around the world beginning with Phoenix AZ and Oslo Norway. These centers will offer professional education for designers to share local influences and styles within an apprentice exchange program and allow tours to anyone looking to see how circularity is already a beautiful and practical part of our world.

In order to create a circular economy that is successful and long lasting, a circular society must be built to support it. To create a circular society, we must change how we think about ourselves and our part in this society. If everyone is a polymath, designer, and problem solver, then we are all given permission to help be part of creating a circular economy and solving today's problems. We are no longer just victims, but active players in the global economy. Circular economy isn't just a small local thing; we are all interconnected in more ways that we realize now. With this new-found power and recognition as problem solvers, we can truly get practical and make changes now.

> "Just as the dandelion pierces through concrete, a person armed with determination can ignite change against the greatest odds and light the way for others."

You are the spark

One of the greatest privileges of leading my company, RENAS AS, is the opportunity to realize the vision of leading the charge to help ignite ideas and businesses to help in the transition toward a circular society. We have been fortunate to be part of helping visionaries establish many firsts in Norway --

- We established Circular Norway in order to help companies and Norwegian society transition toward a Circular Economy.

- We established the start-up Redoit—a platform for businesses and individuals to help change how electronics are owned and used. By taking responsibility for financing, logistics, refurbishment, and recycling, Redoit intends to reduce the significant environmental and economic losses associated with today's linear consumption of electronics.
- We initiated the first Circularity Gap Report in Norway, and we plan to be the first country in the world to launch a follow-up Circularity Gap Report projected for August 2024.
- We have supported dialogue in Norway and around the world in transition to adopt circular principals in policies and businesses.
- We established the adoption of Madaster Services Norway, originally from the Netherlands in 2017, which entails a digital registry for construction materials and products in buildings.
- We support R&D and new innovations for better waste management and recycling practices.
- We support and invest in Li-Tech. With a focus on curbing fires caused by flammable lithium batteries, Li-Tech uses unique sensory data to accurately pinpoint these potential hazards.
- We are committed to actively supporting and advancing efficient Extended Producer Responsibility (EPR) solutions while taking a comprehensive approach to supply chains. Our focus spans from the initial design and sourcing stages to end-of-life treatment.

We believe in the power of collaboration, open dialogue, and listening to the visionaries with their grand ideas. Our role is to help cultivate these futuristic ideas in the present and make the impact needed to push toward a circular economy.

Throughout the years, many grand ideas and start-ups have fallen by the wayside, yet many have been very fruitful and changed the trajectory of Norwegian society. For instance, when we started Circular Norway in 2017, few were talking much about the circular economy. Together with a stellar team, we invested in an informational campaign to raise awareness about the importance of changing our business models away from the linear economy. Now, the concept of the circular economy has become mainstream in Norway, where the discussion is no longer what it is rather than what can we do to become circular.

What I have learned from the leaders who see before we see and do before we do is that they are comfortable with going against the grain and comfortable standing alone. They are confident that their vision will drive them and that eventually others will follow.

I find George Serafeim's book, "Purpose + Profit" very insightful. He shares his insight that alignment is not static, but dynamic. We change. Just see how the pandemic changed our values and our way of living. Many ideas we had before the pandemic are no longer relevant.

What I appreciate about George is that he eloquently shows that external misalignment with your values is not inherently immoral or negative. When offering advice to young individuals, George even proposes the idea of working for a company that is misaligned with their values. His rationale? "The reason is that alignment is not static. Alignment changes over the course of months and years, and it is not entirely out of our control. We have the power to push an organization in a different direction."[130]

He explains that one can initially work at a place, like a nonprofit focused on a passion, and find alignment with their goals. However, over time, that alignment might not progress and could even diminish as both the individual and the organization evolve. On the other side of the spectrum, someone might join a company that initially seems misaligned with their values. Yet, with time and effort, that individual has the potential to change the company's direction, improving its performance and gradually bringing it in tandem with their own values.[131]

What he describes is slow change moving toward the goal. Eventually, the minority becomes the twenty-five percent and then changes the fabric of society.

I resonate with George when he states, "In fact, my intuition says that the world is better off if skilled, passionate business leaders join misaligned organization (ones with a plausible path for improvement) rather than ones already behaving this way."

And it is not just business leaders, but all of us. We can all contribute to change something that seems impossible with our actions. What is key is to be thoughtful and reflect upon where you want to make an impact. The bottom line is that you can change your surroundings with your actions. What I always tell my kids is that,

> **"Your environment will shape you, but your actions will define you."**

Action defines who we are, and the practical step is to take one small action at a time to align the world with circular principles.

conclusion

"It always seems impossible until it's done.".",

-NELSON MANDELA

WE HAVE COME to the end of the book, and I hope I have inspired you to see that one small idea, one small plan, and one small action can lead to real change. If we all take that small action, it leads to a collective impact When we put this into a collaborative context, we can change society. Any transformation will always start with a single action somewhere.

We just need to make sure we have the right goal and vision to move forward.

"Individually, we are one drop. Together, we are an ocean."

- RYUNOSUKE SATORO, *writer, poet*

Even though it is in my nature to strive to be the absolute best that I can be, my main goal is still to find what is beneficial for everyone. **ME is never at the expense of WE.** Upon entering the armed forces, individuals swiftly grasp the fundamental principle – There is no 'I' in team – through military leadership training. Service members promptly learn that fostering cooperation and uniting the team is one of the most important qualities to creating great accomplishments.

Serving in the military was a natural goal in my search for challenge and meaning. Even though I did not make it into the Navy Seals, I was in the US Navy and embodied the SEAL ETHOS code. What is the SEAL ETHOS? *Collaboration, boldness, honesty, loyalty, leadership, humbleness, humility, always in, always learning, and commitment (never fail).* These are the values that inspire great progress. These are the values that can help to drive the circular economy.

The synergy between the small actions of one individual and the greater actions we can take together leads to great things. Together, we can make a better planet for the future of our children and grandchildren. Ask yourself, how can I be a contributing factor to securing nature, the environment, and our resources for future generations?

The impossible can happen. We are at the dawn of the circular life. I believe there are more than twenty-five percent of us who believe it can happen. We are ready for

action and will soldier toward the goal.

In unity, we rise for the collective dream. Let's stand tall and be the spark to drive the circular economy and leave a positive and lasting legacy.

We need to start a conversation with our partners, neighbors, and children, raising awareness and educating them about the needs and consequences of our actions. The goal should be to foster open and honest discussions where everyone and all opinions are invited and respected. Only through such debate and honing of opinions can we achieve real and lasting success.

Sustainability and circular practices should be taught in schools on par with core subjects such as mathematics and language arts. It's essential for long-standing forums and conferences that have addressed these issues for decades to reassess their approach. This is pivotal in our pursuit of preserving nature while simultaneously fostering economic growth and maintaining our quality of life.

Our regulators will not take on the move toward a circular economy unless there is substantial pressure to do so. We have spent hundreds of years perfecting linearity, and we consumers are trained and nudged to respond in certain ways. However, if we keep the conversation going, industry, producers, and regulators will respond to the sentiments of consumers. If we take the lead, others will follow and inspire more people. This is the ripple effect of change. This is win for all, and simply put, smart business.

So, what are some effective and practical approaches we can take to ignite action toward a circular economy?

It begins with asking yourself:

"What's in it for me today?"
"What's in it for me over five years?"
"What's in it for me over my lifetime?"
"What's in it for me through my grandchild's lifetime?"

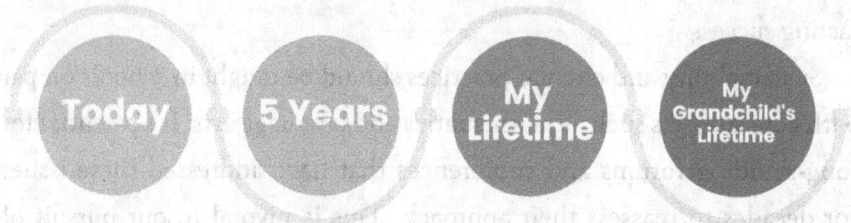

epilogue

My passion for finding the right words to inspire action and to adopt a circular mindset continues.

The greatest danger right now is the lack of full understanding of the power of a circular economic mindset--the belief we can make a change and inspire full adoption worldwide.

And yet we are closer than we think...

We are united more than we think...

It is easy to believe that we are fighting an uphill battle when, in fact, there is an army of people ready to do their part.

Case in point, as a partner of the Nexus Council with its mission to build bridges, we conducted research in the fall of 2023 on the state of understanding the circular economy. We did this by conducting a survey on language as it relates to environmental discussion with 1000 American adults.

I found it intriguing that the circular economy concept was largely unfamiliar to most

Americans. However, upon providing a clear definition, as outlined in this book, three out of four Americans expressed wholehearted support for the circular economy and a desire to take more action. Even more intriguing is that it garners broad bipartisan support among Americans who were previously unaware of it.

This leads me to the question: What obstacles stand in our way of embracing it? From a bird's eye view, there is no single or easy answer to this question. But I believe the answer lies in the words we choose and how we employ them. The unfamiliarity with the term circular economy among most Americans underscores the lack of clear, effective communication. When we define and articulate these concepts comprehensively, we bridge the knowledge gap and create a shared understanding, unlocking the potential for widespread support and the potential for change.

Changing systems on a societal level can at first feel like an overwhelming task and lead to apathy and despair, but, as we have discussed throughout the book, we need just to downsize this to our personal level and ask ourselves "how do we eat an elephant?" Many of us know this question and will immediately reply "one bite at a time." See, it's as easy as pie.

acknowledgments

I WOULD LIKE TO EXPRESS my sincere gratitude to all the wonderful people who have helped me on the journey of writing this book.

Thanks to all my colleagues, coworkers, and good advisors for great conversations and discussions about the different aspects of circularity, sustainability, and life in general.

Thanks to the team Torund Bryhn, JJ Brown, Ian Peterman, Zachary Houghton, Sage Toomey, Lisa Duncan, and Heidi Stangeland for their invaluable feedback and guidance.

To Ingvil Gaasland and Ellen Høvik for their insightful comments and encouragement.

Special thanks to my voice writer Torund Bryhn for making this happen, for her help with research, writing, bringing in new angles and perspectives, and helping me get my voice on paper.

Thank you to my right-hand people: Frank Jaegtnes, Leif Nordhus, and Alexander Christiansen. I truly appreciate you constructively challenging my ideas and perspectives. Our discussions are reflected throughout the book.

To my readers, I want to extend my sincere and honest thanks to every one of you. You have been my constant source of motivation, and I hope you enjoy reading this book and are left with a sense of inspiration when you turn the last page.

Finally, a monumental thanks to my wife Live and sons Marcus and Christopher for your unwavering patience and support. You are the best.

I could list hundreds more thank yous, but I'd have to publish a whole second book to fit them all. Even if I did this, I'm sure I would still forget someone, but you know who you are and I thank you.

> ## "I can no other answer make but thanks, And thanks; and ever thanks;"
>
> --Sebastian. Shakespeare, *Twelfth Night,* Act III, Scene 3

about the author

BJØRN ARILD THON

Bjørn Arild Thon has been a steadfast advocate in the recycling and circular economy domain. With over 20 years in the industry, he was appointed to RENAS, Norway's premier recycling enterprise, in 2014, where he has since worked diligently to bring the ideals of the circular economy from theory to application within businesses and governmental organizations.

In addition to his role at RENAS, Thon played a crucial role in the establishment of Circular Norway, an organization aimed at promoting circular economy principles. Motivated by the 2018 Circularity Gap Report, he was instrumental in presenting Norway's inaugural Circularity Report in 2020, underlining Norway's commitment to this sustainable approach.

Thon also lent his support to Redoit, an initiative centered on giving a new lease of life to electronics. Seeing the success of the Netherlands-based Madaster, he recognized the potential of cataloging materials used in construction, and thus championed this idea within Norway.

In 2022, through a collaboration with The ONS Conference, Thon contributed to the initiation of the energy sector's first survey concerning the circular economy. This endeavor provided essential insights into the industry's perspective, leading to his appointment on the ONS Energy Society Committee board.

Furthermore, Thon was involved in the early stages of Skift: Business Climate Leaders network. This initiative, collaborating with over sixty of Norway's notable companies, underscores the significant role businesses can play in a green transition. As a representative for both Skift and RENAS, Thon has consistently engaged with leaders in the field, emphasizing the significance of the circular economy for Norway's sustainable future.

The Contributors

J.J. Brown

JJ dedicated nearly 20 years to shaping policy alongside Senator Orrin G. Hatch on Capitol Hill. Specializing in the intricate workings of the Congressional process, he championed landmark initiatives, most notably uniting disparate sectors for the Energy Policy Act of 2005, promoting alternative vehicle tax credits. Additionally, his cross-aisle strategies birthed the 2007 plug-in vehicle tax credit and all tax incentives for carbon capture projects. After leaving the Senate, JJ has imparted his legislative expertise as an adjunct professor at George Washington University and Southern Virginia University. Recognized as a leading voice on national policy strategy, he's been invited to speak from Mexico City to Monaco and various US venues.

Torund Bryhn

Torund Bryhn, is the Executive Director of the NEXUS Council, and the founder of Diotima Strategies and St. John's Press. She stands out as a visionary in blending communication with impactful environmental action. With roots in energy, Carbon Capture and Storage (CCS), arts, public policy, and foreign affairs, Bryhn's two-decades-long experience has enabled organizations to redefine their narratives and reputations. Recognizing the critical importance of the circular economy during the COVID-19 pandemic, Bryhn collaborated with RENAS, Norway's leading electronic waste recycling firm, to devise communication strategies that resonated with the masses, emphasizing a sustainable future. With a Master's from Columbia University and a heart rooted in the arts and politics, Bryhn continues her quest for a sustainable world by championing effective communication and inclusive dialogue.

Ian Peterman

Ian Peterman is leading the way for Conscious Design thinking through his book, podcast, and public appearances. His methods for prioritizing restorative, sustainable, and inclusive values to build a legacy of positive impact for his client's brands has offered an exciting and rewarding approach to the future of good business. The Peterman Design Firm specializes in developing and commercializing products and offers branding and marketing for the missions his clients create. Ian also builds teams and catalyzes growth via fractional COO and CMO services. Ian is passionate about green tech, space exploration, and creating meaningful connections through human centered planet friendly brands. When he's not teaching and implementing Conscious Design he enjoys family, food, and watching the night sky. To learn more about Ian and Conscious Design, you can check out @Petermanfirm for the latest podcasts, projects, and events, or find his book, *Conscious Design*, on Amazon.

resources

Recommended Reading

Reports:

- European Commission. "European Green Deal." https://ec.europa.eu/info/strategy/priorities-2019-2024/european-green-deal_en.

- European Environment Agency. "Circular Economy Action Plan." https://environment.ec.europa.eu/strategy/circular-economy-action-plan_en.

- Climate Technology Centre & Network. "Assessment of the current status of Circular Economy." https://www.ctc-n.org/technical-assistance/projects/assessment-current-status-circular-economy-developing-roadmap.

- World Economic Forum. "Companies leading the way to a Circular Economy." February, 2019. https://www.weforum.org/agenda/2019/02/companies-leading-way-to-circular-economy/.

- Circle Economy Foundation. https://www.circle-economy.com

- Ellen MacArthur Foundation. "Introduction to the Circular Economy: Overview." https://ellenmacarthurfoundation.org/topics/circular-economy-introduction/overview.

- Circularity Gap. https://www.circularity-gap.world.

- Our World in Data. https://ourworldindata.org/.

notes

Notes on the Usage of AI Tools:

With the emergence of ChatGPT and other AI tools, it is necessary to indicate when AI is used, yet the preferred method of doing so is still evolving. In this book, we followed the guidelines in the Chicago Manual of Style:

Chat GPT:

- Translation: ChatGPT was the first resource we used for translating the interviews that were conducted for the editor to review. Many parts of the book were originally written in Norwegian.
- Encyclopedia and dictionary: Since ChatGPT is user-friendly for locating dates, definitions, and synonyms, it became my go-to resource. From there, I validated the information with reliable sources such as the Merriam-Webster dictionary for definitions, Britannica for key historical dates and references, and other books as needed.

Grammarly:

- Editing: As grammar and punctuation are two of my weaknesses when it comes to writing, most of the text in the book would go through Grammarly before I engaged an editor.

Scribbr:

- Plagiarism: The book has gone through the AI tool for detecting plagiarism. This is to ensure that I have cited all sources.

Introduction

1   Zoe Tabary. "Waste is 'worth gold', city dwellers told in push to reuse resources." Reuters. Published May 23, 20219. Accessed September 27, 2023. https://www.reuters.com/article/global-environment-cities/waste-is-worth-gold-city-dwellers-told-in-push-to-reuse-resources-idUKL5N22Z576.

2   "Introduction to the Circular Economy." Ellen MacArthur Foundation. Accessed October 2, 2023. https://www.ellenmacarthurfoundation.org/topics/circular-economy-introduction/overview.

3   IEA, "The Role of Critical World Energy Outlook Special Report Minerals in Clean Energy Transitions" Last modified March 2022. May 2021. Accessed August 22, 2022 https://www.iea.org/reports/the-role-of-critical-minerals-in-clean-energy-transitions/executive-summary.

4   SINTEF, "Annual and Sustainability Report 2022," Published May 2023. Accessed August 29, 2023. https://www.sintef.no/en/sintef-group/annual-reports-and-brochures/annual-and-sustainability-report-2022/.

5   SINTEF, Annual Report, 66-67.

6   SINTEF, Annual Report, 66-67.

7   SINTEF, Annual Report, 66-67.

8   Oliver Franklin-Wallis, "Wasteland" (Hachette Books, New York, 2023), p xx cited World Economic Forum, "A New Circular Vision." 11.

9   Franklin-Wallis, "Wasteland" 249.

10   Erik Osmundsen. "Det finnes ikke søppel mer - NHOs årskonferanse 2017." YouTube, uploaded January 5, 2017, http://www.youtube.com/watch?v=Atft1eHC36Y.

11   President von der Leyen, "A Union that Stands Strong Together." State of the Union Address. Strasbourg. September 14, 2022. https://e.europa.eu/commission/presscorner/detail/en/speech_22_5493

12   Bernadette Giacomazzo."The Bizarre History Of The Mongoose In Hawaii And Why Colonial Sugar Barons Are To Blame For The Havoc It's Caused." ATI. Published June 22, 2022. Accessed September 26, 2023. https://allthatsinteresting.com/mongoose-in-hawaii.

CHAPTER ONE: Origins of Our Dilemmas

13   Avinash Dixit. "Paul Samuelson's Legacy." Accessed September 1, 2023. Princeton University - Written for the *Annual Review of Economics*, Vol. 4, 2012. https://www.princeton.edu/~dixitak/home/PASLegacy2_WP.pdf

14   Abdulkader Cassim, Mahomedya. "Public Policy in Islamic Framework: Exploring Paradigm based on Islamic Epistemology." (2015). https://doi.org/10.22373/share.v4i2.1030.

15   Thomas Demuynck and Per Hjertstrand. "Samuelson's Approach to Revealed Preference
Theory: Some Recent Advances." Accessed September 3, 2023. Published 2019. https://www.ifn.se/wfiles/wp/wp1274.pdf.

16   Wikipedia, s.v. "Paul Samuelson." Last modified 27 August 2023 . Accessed September 3, 2023. https://en.wikipedia.org/wiki/Paul_Samuelson.

17   Kate Raworth. "Doughnut Economics: Seven Ways to Think Like a 21st-Century Economist." London: Random House, 2017. Kindle Location: 376.

18   Yara Simón. "Who Invented the Assembly Line?" Science: How Stuff Works. Accessed January 26, 2024. https://science.howstuffworks.com/innovation/inventions/who-invented-the-assembly-line.htm#:~:text=While%20Henry%20Ford%20didn't,when%20producing%20the%20Model%20T.&text=The%20use%20of%20interchangeable%20parts,and%20speed%20never%20seen%20before.

19   Michael Marcin, "Resource Light: History of the Assembly Line: Evolution of Efficiency." Crest Capital website. Accessed January 26, 2024. https://www.crestcapital.com/tax/history_of_the_assembly_line#:~:text=The%20assembly%20line%20has%20revolutionized,development%2C%20and%20the%20global%20economy.

20   Samuel Strauss . "Things are in the Saddle." *Atlantic Monthly*. Published November 1924. Accessed August 2023. https://www.theatlantic.com/magazine/archive/1924/11/things-are-in-the-saddle/648025/.

21   Jeansonne Glen. "Secretary of Commerce, Locomotive of the Economy." *A Life Herbert Hoover* (Berkley: New American Library) 153-185.

22   Kendrik A. Clements. "Consumption and Conservation." *Hoover, conservation, and consumerism: Engineering the good life*. (Lawrence: University Press of Kansas, 2000). 41 – 59.

23   Khan Academy. "1920s consumption." Accessed September 3, 2023. https://www.khanacademy.org/humanities/us-history/rise-to-world-power/1920s-america/a/1920s-consumption.

24   Larry Tye. "Father of Spin Edward L. Bernays and the Birth of Public Relations." (New York: Henry Holt and Company LLC, 1998).

25   President Calvin Coolidge. "Address Before the American Association of Advertising Agencies in Washington, D.C." October 27, 1926. Accessed September 1, 2023. https://www.presidency.ucsb.edu/documents/address-before-the-american-association-advertising-agencies-washington-dc.

26   The Museum of Public Relations. "Pioneer - Edward Bernays." Accessed September 2, 2023. https://www.prmuseum.org/pioneer-edward-bernays.

27   "Politicians used Freudian ideas to first convince Americans they needed capitalism." Quartz. Published May 7, 2017. Accessed September 2, 2023. https://qz.com/976472/politicians-used-freudian-ideas-to-first-convince-americans-they-needed-capitalism.

28   Adam Curtis, "The Century of Self" (BBC FOUR Aired Monday April, 29 – Thursday, May 2, 2002)YouTube Accessed: September 2, 2023.

29   Gus Lubin. "There's A Staggering Conspiracy Behind The Rise Of Consumer Culture." *Business Insider*. Published Feb 23, 2013. Accessed September 2, 2023. https://www.businessinsider.com/birth-of-consumer-culture-2013-2.

30   Paul C. Hutton."The Shift from Sustainable to Regenerative Design." Sustainable Brands. Accessed December 4, 2023. "https://sustainablebrands.com/read/product-service-design-innovation/sustainable-regenerative-design.

31   Brian H Roberts. "The Application of Industrial Ecology Principles and Planning Guidelines for the Development of Eco-Industrial Parks." Research Gate. https://www.researchgate.net/figure/Basic-Concepts-of-Industrial-Ecology_fig1_223004844.

32   Franklin-Wallis, "Wasteland." 6

33   Franklin-Wallis, "Wasteland." 39

34   Franklin-Wallis, "Wasteland." 19

35   Franklin-Wallis, "Wasteland." 4

36   Franklin-Wallis, "Wasteland" p 248 – the gold was calculated by the author using

Apple, "Environmental Responsibility Report; 2019 Progress report, covering fiscal year 2018. https://www.apple.com/environment/pdf/Apple_Environmental_Responsibility_Report_2019.pdf

37   Franklin-Wallis, "Wasteland." 248

38   Franklin-Wallis, "Wasteland." 248

39   Regína Hrönn Ragnarsdóttir. "The Study Centre on Leader-Sheep in North-East Iceland – The Unique Breed of Icelandic Sheep." *Guide To Iceland*. Accessed September 4, 2023. https://guidetoiceland.is/connect-with-locals/regina/the-study-centre-on-leader-wethers.

40   99Science – Ghana's Leading Scicomm platform. "Sheep flock–follow the leader wherever they go." Accessed September 4, 2023. https://99science.org/2021/01/04/sheep-flock-follow-the-leader-wherever-the-go/#:~:text=Leadersheep%20are%20a%20strain%20of,superior%20ability%20to%20sense%20danger.

CHAPTER TWO: The Barrier to Change . . . Is Change

41   Kim Borg and Bradley Jorgensen. "Big issue' documentaries don't always change our behaviour." *Phys Org*, Published August 15, 2017. Accessed September 4, 2023. https://phys.org/news/2017-08-big-issue-documentaries-dont-behaviour.html.

42   Donald Miller. "Building a StoryBrand" (Nashville: Harper Collins Leadership, 2017) 6-14.

43   Miller. "StoryBrand" 6-14.

44   Hugo Mercier and Dan Sperber. "Enigma of Reason" (Cambridge Massachusetts: Harvard University Press, 2017)

45   Circle Economy and Circular Norway. "The Circularity Gap Report Norway." Published August 2020. https://www.circularity-gap.world/norway.

46   Ryan W. Hirsch. "Why Denzel Washington Wants Reporters to Tell the Truth." The NASBA Center for the Public Trust (CPT). Accessed September 19, 2023. https://thecpt.org/2016/12/19/why-denzel-washington-wants-reporters-to-tell-the-truth/.

47   Andrew McKay. "Black Gold: Norway's Oil Story." *Life in Norway*. Published October 2, 2019. Accessed September 19, 2023. https://www.lifeinnorway.net/norway-oil-history/.

48   Ministry of Petroleum and Energy and the Norwegian Petroleum Directorate. "Exports of Oil and Gas." NORWEGIANPETROLEUM.NO. Accessed September 19, 2023. https://www.norskpetroleum.no/en/production-and-exports/exports-of-oil-and-gas/#:~:text=Combined%2C%20oil%20and%20gas%20exceeds,commodities%20in%20the%20Norwegian%20economy/.

49   Sigmnd Størset. "Industrial opportunities and employment prospects in large-scale CO_2 management in Norway." #SINTEFblog. Published May 3, 2028. Accessed September 19, 2023. https://blog.sintef.com/sintefenergy/ccs/industrial-opportunities-and-employment-prospects-in-large-scale-co2-management-in-norway/.

50   Jack Ewing. "In Norway, the Electric Vehicle Future Has Already Arrived." *The New York Times*. Updated September 17, 2023. Accessed September 19, 2023. https://www.nytimes.com/2023/05/08/business/energy-environment/norway-electric-vehicles.html.

51   Shara Mabast Ali, Emil Yde Aasen, Katrine Haram Olsen, Eyolf Strømme-Svendsen, and Saresh Mohamad "Four reasons. "Why young people don't bother listening to the oil and gas industry" Norwegian Oil and Gas Association. Published 2016. https://www.offshorenorge.no/globalassets/dokumenter/den-nye-oljen---english-summary.pdf.

CHAPTER THREE: We have done it before

52   RENAS AS and ONS Foundation, "Survey Report: A Journey Towards a Circular Economy" Published September 2022. https://nexuscouncil.org/wp-content/uploads/2023/08/Transitioning-to-a-Circular-Economy.pdf.

53   UN Environment Programme. "Rebuilding the ozone layer: how the world came together for the ultimate repair job." Published September 15, 2021. Accessed September 16, 2023. https://www.unep.org/news-and-stories/story/rebuilding-ozone-layer-how-world-came-together-ultimate-repair-job.

54   UN Environment Programme. "Rebuilding the ozone layer: how the world came together for the ultimate repair job." Published September 15, 2021. Accessed September 16, 2023. https://www.unep.org/news-and-stories/story/rebuilding-ozone-layer-how-world-came-together-ultimate-repair-job.

55   UN Environment Programme. "Rebuilding the ozone layer: how the world came together for the ultimate repair job." Published September 15, 2021. Accessed September 16, 2023. https://www.unep.org/news-and-stories/story/rebuilding-ozone-layer-how-world-came-together-ultimate-repair-job.

56   Fisheres. "Fishing the River Thames in Greater London" Accessed August 31, 2023 https://www.fisheries.co.uk/london/#:~:text=Fishing%20the%20River%20Thames%20 in,the%20best%20places%20to%20fish.

57   UN Environment Programme. "Montreal Protocol: fixing the ozone layer and reducing climate change." Published September 16, 2023. Accessed September 16, 2023 https://ozone.unep.org/ozone-day/montreal-protocol-fixing-the-zone-layer-and-reducing-climate-change.

58   UNECE: Environment Policy: Air Pollution. "The Convention and its achievements." Accessed August 31, 2023. https://unece.org/convention-and-its-achievements.

59   Henry Fountain and John Schwartz. "CLIMATE FWD: Have We Passed the Acid Test?" Published May 2, 2018. Accessed August 31, 2023. https://www.nytimes.com/2018/05/02/climate/climate-fwd-acid-rain.html.

60   Damon Centola, Joshua Becker, Devon Brackbill, and Andrea Baronchelli. "Experimental evidence for tipping
points in social convention." *Science Magazine*. Published. June 8, 2018. Accessed September 19, 2023, via Annenberg School of Communications. https://www.asc.upenn.edu/ sites/default/files/2021-03/Experimental%20evidence%20for%20tipping%20points%20 in%20social%20convention.pdf.

61   IKEA. "Reuse, resell or recycle – how we enable circular services." Accessed Sept 19, 2023. https://www.ikea.com/global/en/our-business/people-planet/circular-services/.

CHAPTER FOUR: Solutions

62   "The Dangers of Linear Thinking in a World of Complexity." https://www.intelligentmanagement.ws/dangers-linear-thinking-world-of-complexity/.

63   Design Declaration Summit. "The Montreal Design Declaration." Published October 24, 2017. Accessed August 31, 2023. https://www.designdeclaration.org/declaration/.

65   EU Science Hub. "Sustainable Product Policy." https://joint-research-centre.ec.europa.eu/scientific-activities-z/sustainable-product-policy_en.

66   Takeda. "Reducing environmental impact through product design and packaging." Accessed September 4, 2023. https://jobs.takeda.com/sustainability-by-design#:~:-text=Reducing%20environmental%20impact%20through%20product,phase%20of%20 that%20product's%20development.

67   Ian Peterman and Jessica Peterman. "Conscious Design" (Insight Technical Educa-tion, October 28, 2021) https://www.amazon.com/Conscious-Design-Ian-Peterman-eb-ook/dp/B09KNMN9BT/ref=sr_1_2?keywords=ian+peterman+conscious+design&-qid=1695150136&s=amazon-devices&sr=1-2.

68   Equo International, accessed September 27, 2023, https://equo-intl.myshopify.com/. https://equo-intl.myshopify.com/.

69   "Restore TC: Recovery Comfort Shoes," Hoka, Accessed September 27, 2023, https://www.hoka.com/en/us/recovery-comfort-shoes/restore-tc/1134532.htm-l?dwvar_1134532_color=OMSO.

70   Katie Baron, "Hoka One One: The Anatomy Of Sports' Fastest Growing, Cri-sis-Proof Sneaker Star," *Forbes*, June 26, 2020, https://www.forbes.com/sites/katiebar-on/2020/06/26/hoka-one-one-the-anatomy-of-sports-fastest-growing-cris.

71   "Green Building Program" City of Scottsdale Website. Accessed December 4, 2023. https://www.scottsdaleaz.gov/green-building-program.

72   "City of Scottsdale General Plan Annual Report January – December 2022." City of Scottsdale. www.scottsdaleaz.gov/Assets/ScottsdaleAZ/General+Plan/2035/Gener-al+Plan+Annual+Report+2022.pdf.

73   Tracy Brower, PhD, Senior Contributor. "Boost Productivity 20%: The Surprising Power Of Play." *Forbes*. Published March 3, 2019. Accessed September 6, 2023. https://www.forbes.com/sites/tracybrower/2019/03/03/boost-productivity-20-the-surpris-ing-power-of-play/?sh=3eb7d3117c05.

74   "Car Allowance Rebate System." Wikipedia. Accessed December 4, 2023. https://en.wikipedia.org/wiki/Car_Allowance_Rebate_System.

75   Finn Arne Jørgensen, Making a Green Machine: The Infrastructure of Beverage Container Recycling, Rutgers University Press.

76   Eve Tahmincioglu. "Remember the Milkman? In Some Places, He's Back." *The New York Times* December 16, 2027. https://www.nytimes.com/2007/12/16/business/your-money/16milk.html?ex=1355461200.

77   Matthew Taylor. "Can Norway help us solve the plastic crisis, one bottle at a time?" *The Guardian*. Published July 12, 2018. Accessed September 11, 2023. https://www.theguardian.com/environment/2018/jul/12/can-norway-help-us-solve-the-plastic-crisis-one-bottle-at-a-time.

78   Matthew Taylor. "Can Norway help us solve the plastic crisis, one bottle at a time?"

The Guardian. Published July 12, 2018. Accessed September 11, 2023. https://www.theguardian.com/environment/2018/jul/12/can-norway-help-us-solve-the-plastic-crisis-one-bottle-at-a-time.

79   "Sensor technology: How tiny technology makes a big environmental impact." TOMRA website. June 9, 2023 Accessed Jan, 25, 2024. https://www.tomra.com/en/reverse-vending/media-center/feature-articles/sensor-technology

80   Jørgensen. "Making a Green Machine."

81   Seinfeld Clips. "The 9999 Bottle & Cans - Seinfeld Shortened Episode." Aired May 2, 1996. Accessed September 11, 2023. https://www.youtube.com/watch?v=bGJZcHgqX-1g&t=111s.

82   National Council of State Legislatures. "State Beverage Container Deposit Laws." Revised March 13, 2020. Accessed. September 11, 2023. https://www.ncsl.org/environment-and-natural-resources/state-beverage-container-deposit-laws.

83   Jørgensen. "Making a Green Machine."

84   Jørgensen. "Making a Green Machine."

85   "About TOMRA." TOMRA Website.Accessed December 4, 2023. https://www.tomra.com/en/about-tomra

86   OECD. "Extended Producer Responsibility." Accessed January 29, 2024. https://www.oecd.org/environment/extended-producer-responsibility.htm:

87   Åge Mariussen and Finn Ørstavik. "Innsikter og anbefalinger fra forskning om klynger og klyngepolitikk" Nordisk institutt for studier av innovasjon, forskning og utdanning. Published September 20, 2005. Accessed September 23, 2023. https://nifu.brage.unit.no/nifu-xmlui/handle/11250/283405.

88   Anders Vinnogg. "Startskuddet har gått i europeisk batteriindustri, og vi må koble oss tettere på andre europeiske land." Innovation Norway. Published. Accessed September 26, 2023. https://www.innovasjonnorge.no/artikkel/startskuddet-har-gatt-i-europeisk-batteriindustri-og-vi-ma-koble-oss-tettere-pa-andre-europeiske-land.

89   Warren Tenney."Purified Recycled Water: City of Scottsdale Innovation Turns 20." The Arizona Municipal Water Users Association website. December 17, 2018. https://www.amwua.org/blog/purified-recycled-water-city-of-scottsdale-innovation-turns-20

90   Claire Fahy. "Would You Drink Wastewater? What if It Was Beer?" *New York Times.* Published June 22, 2023. https://www.nytimes.com/2023/07/22/business/beer-recycled-wastewater.html

91   City of Scottsdale. "Advanced Water Purification." Accessed September 19, 2023. https://www.scottsdaleaz.gov/water/recycled-water.

CHAPTER FIVE: Igniting the Momentum: Finance and Government in the Push for Sustainability

92   Duke University. "In the race of life, the tortoise beats the hare every time: Research shows that, when speed is averaged throughout a lifetime, the fastest animals and machines are actually the slowest." *Science Daily*. Published August 27, 2018. Accessed September 6, 2023, www.sciencedaily.com/releases/2018/08/180827080908.htm

93   A. Bejan, U. Gunes, J. D. Charles & B. Sahin. "The fastest animals and vehicles are neither the biggest nor the fastest over lifetime." *Scientific Reports*. Published. Accessed September 19, 2023. https://www.nature.com/articles/s41598-018-30303-1.

94   1934: The Securities Exchange Act of 1934 established the U.S. Securities and Exchange Commission (SEC) and introduced key reporting and disclosure requirements for publicly traded companies, primarily centered on annual reports.

95   George Serefim, "Purpose + Profit: How Business can life up the world." (Harper Collins Leadership, Nashville 2022) p.6.

96   NG Group. "Annual Report 2022 Norsk Gjenvinning Norge AS." Published May 16, 2023. Accessed September 25, 2023. https://www.nggroup.no/media/2091/ngn-group-consolidated-financial-statement-2023-incl-audit-report.pdf.

97   Barbara DeLollis. "Trash to treasure: How one CEO is disrupting a legacy industry to save the planet." May 12, 2023. https://www.hbs.edu/bigs/blog/post/trash-to-treasure.

98   Adrian Dearnell. "Are You Ready For An Integrated Annual Report?" *Forbes*. Published December 20, 2022. Accessed September 28, 2023. https://www.forbes.com/sites/adriandearnell/2022/12/20/are-you-ready-for-an-integrated-annual-report/?sh=6d519e114ec2.

CHAPTER SIX: The Acceleration of Sustainability

99   Integrated Reporting. "About Us." Accessed September 25, 2023. https://www.integratedreporting.org/the-iirc-2/.

100   Stephanie Brinley. "EV Chargers: How many do we need?" *SP Global Mobility*. Published January 9, 2023. Accessed: September 23, 2023. https://www.spglobal.com/mobility/en/research-analysis/ev-chargers-how-many-do-we-need.html.

101   Jeff Siegel. "90% of all Cars Sold Last Month Were Electric." *Energy & Capital*. Published July 10, 2023. Accessed September 23, 2023. https://www.energyandcapital.com/articles/90-of-all-cars-sold-last-month-were-electric/112927#:~:text=Well%2C%20the%20numbers%20are%20in,the%20total%20new%20car%20sales.

102   J.B. Straubel. "Written Testimony: The scope and scale of critical mineral demand and recycling of critical minerals." Senate Energy Committee on Energy and Natural Resources. Published April 7, 2022. Accessed September 23, 2023. https://www.energy.senate.gov/services/files/43143C20-B0B4-4BC7-A5E2-5B2CB2CDE4D2.

103   Daisy Simmons."Don't get fossil fooled: EVs really are better for the climate." *The Driven*. Published November 9, 2022. Accessed September 23, 2023. https://thedriven.io/2022/11/09/dont-get-fossil-fooled-evs-really-are-better-for-the-climate/.

104   European Commission: Single Market and Standards. "Critical raw materials." Published 2023. Accessed September 23, 2023. https://single-market-economy.ec.europa.eu/sectors/raw-materials/areas-specific-interest/critical-raw-materials_en.

105   Jocelyn C. Zuckerman. "For Your Phone and EV, a Cobalt Supply Chain to a Hell on Earth." *Yale Environment* 360. Published March 30, 2023. Accessed September 23, 2023. https://e360.yale.edu/features/siddharth-kara-cobalt-mining-labor-congo.

106   U.S. Department of Energy. "Biden-Harris Administration Announces $30 Million to Build Up Domestic Supply Chain for Critical Minerals." Energy.gov. Published August 21, 2023. Accessed September 23, 2023. https://www.energy.gov/articles/biden-harris-administration-announces-30-million-build-domestic-supply-chain-critical#:~:text=WASHINGTON%2C%20D.C.%20%E2%80%94%20In%20support%20of,-from%20domestic%20coal%2Dbased%20resources.

107   Amy Lv and Dominique Patton. "China exported no germanium, gallium in August after export curbs." Reuters. Published September 20, 2023. Accessed September 23, 2023. https://www.reuters.com/world/china/china-exported-no-germanium-gallium-aug-due-export-curbs-2023-09-20/.

108   European Commission: Single Market and Standards. "Critical raw materials." Published 2023. Accessed September 23, 2023. https://single-market-economy.ec.europa.eu/sectors/raw-materials/areas-specific-interest/critical-raw-materials_en.

109   U.S. Department of Energy. "Biden-Harris Administration Announces $30 Million to Build Up Domestic Supply Chain for Critical Minerals." Energy.gov. Pub-

lished August 21, 2023. Accessed September 23, 2023. https://www.energy.gov/articles/
biden-harris-administration-announces-30-million-build-domestic-supply-chain-crit-
ical#:~:text=WASHINGTON%2C%20D.C.%20%E2%80%94%20In%20support%20of,-
from%20domestic%20coal%2Dbased%20resources.

110   Rare Earth Magnet: This refers to a type of permanent magnet made from alloys
of rare earth elements. They are known for their ability to have very high magnetic fields
and retain their magnetism. The two main types of rare earth magnets are neodymium
magnets (made from an alloy of neodymium, iron, and boron) and samarium-cobalt
magnets.

111   European Commission: Single Market and Standards. "Critical raw materials."
Published 2023. Accessed September 23, 2023. https://single-market-economy.ec.europa.
eu/sectors/raw-materials/areas-specific-interest/critical-raw-materials_en

112   U.S. Department of Energy: Critical Minerals & Materials Program. "What Are
Critical Materials and Critical Minerals?" Enegy.gov. Published. Accessed September
23, 2023. https://www.energy.gov/cmm/what-are-critical-materials-and-critical-miner-
als#:~:text=Critical%20minerals%3A%20The%20Secretary%20of,%2C%20cobalt%2C%20
dysprosium%2C%20erbium%2C.

113   Francesco La Camera."Geopolitics of the Energy Transition: Critical Materials."
International Renewable Energy Agency https://mc-cd8320d4-36a1-40ac-83cc-3389-
cdn-endpoint.azureedge.net/-/media/Files/IRENA/Agency/Publication/2023/Jul/IRE-
NA_Geopolitics_energy_transition_critical_materials_2023.pdf?rev=420aeb58d2e745d-
79f1b564ea89ef9f8.

114   Jamie Ducharme."The Overlooked Environmental Impact of Vaping." *TIME*.
Published July 11, 2021. Accessed September 23, 2023. https://time.com/6293772/dispos-
able-vapes-plastic-waste/.

115   Yuan Yang, George Parker and Jim Pickard. "The environmental cost of single-use
vapes." *Jaraa'id*. Published March 7, 2023. Accessed September 26, 2023. https://www.
jaraaid.com/business/the-environmental-cost-of-single-use-vapes/.

116   Anuja Majmundar , Zheng Xue , Samuel Asare, and Nigar Nargis. " Trends in
public interest in shopping and point-ofsales of JUUL and Puff Bar 2019–2021." BMJ
Journals. Published May 11, 2022. Accessed September 23, 2023. https://tobaccocontrol.
bmj.com/content/tobaccocontrol/early/2022/04/20/tobaccocontrol-2021-056953.full.
pdf

117   US Food and Drug Administration. "FDA Denies Authorization to Market JUUL
Products." Published June 23, 2022. Accessed September 26, 2023. https://www.fda.gov/
news-events/press-announcements/fda-denies-authorization-market-juul-products.

118   ABC News. "Despite ban, CA's flavored tobacco 'black market alive and well' due to loophole." Published March 31, 2023. Accessed September 26, 2023. https://www.youtube.com/watch?v=EGb1AXOXCf8.

119   Disney. "Friends for Change: Project Green." Accessed January 29, 2024. http://disney.go.com/projectgreen/resourceclimate/

120   Thomas Husson. "Beware The Stereotype: Gen Z Isn't The Most Actively Green Generation." Forrester. April 21, 2023. https://www.forrester.com/blogs/beware-the-stereotype-gen-z-isnt-the-most-actively-green-generation/.

121   William McBride, Alex Muresianu, Garrett Watson. "Changing Trends in R&D Investment Show the Importance of Business R&D." Tax Foundation. Published December 14, 2022. Accessed September 18, 2023. https://taxfoundation.org/data/all/federal/business-r-d-investment-.

122   Alberto Alcalde-Calonge, Francisco José Sáez-Martínez, Pablo Ruiz-Palomino, "Evolution of research on circular economy and related trends and topics. A thirteen-year review, Ecological Informatics, Volume 70, 2022, 101716, ISSN 1574-9541,(https://www.sciencedirect.com/science/article/pii/S1574954122001662) (https://www.sciencedirect.com/science/article/pii/S1574954122001662)

123   "About TOMRA." TOMRA Website. Accessed December 4, 2023. https://www.tomra.com/en/about-tomra.

124   SINTEF, "Annual and Sustainability Report 2022," Published May 2023. Accessed August 29, 2023. https://www.sintef.no/en/sintef-group/annual-reports-and-brochures/annual-and-sustainability-report-2022/.

CHAPTER SEVEN: Collaboration Is the Future

125   "Equinor Doubles Share of Investment in Renewables." *Offshore Engineer*. Published November 9, 2022.. Accessed September 19, 2023. https://www.oedigital.com/news/500801-equinor-doubles-share-of-investment-in-renewables

126   "Administrerende direktør for Skift Norge, Bjørn Kjærand Haugland:Brobygger for det grønne skiftet." Norge i dag. https://idag.no/brobygger-for-det-gronne-skiftet/19.41631.

127   The Norwegian Agency for Public and Financial Management (DFØ). "Action plan to increase the proportion of green public procurements and green innovation." Published 2021. Accessed September 26, 2023. https://www.sustainability.gov/pdfs/ggi-norway.pdf.

128   The Norwegian Agency for Public and Financial Management (DFØ). "Action plan to increase the proportion of green public procurements and green innovation." Published 2021. Accessed September 26, 2023. https://www.sustainability.gov/pdfs/ggi-norway.pdf.

129   The Norwegian Agency for Public and Financial Management (DFØ). "Action plan to increase the proportion of green public procurements and green innovation." Published 2021. Accessed September 26, 2023. https://www.sustainability.gov/pdfs/ggi-norway.pdf.

130   George Serafeim. "Purpose + Profit." (Harper Collins Leadership, Nashville 2023). 148

131   Mahomedya, Abdulkader Cassim. "Public Policy in Islamic Framework: Exploring Paradigm based on Islamic Epistemology." (2015). https://doi.org/10.22373/share.v4i2.1030.

131   Thomas Demuynck and Per Hjertstrand, "Samuelson's Approach to Revealed Preference Theory: Some Recent Advances." Accessed September 3, 2023. Published 2019. https://www.ifn.se/wfiles/wp/wp1274.pdf.

131   George Serafeim. "Purpose + Profit." (Harper Collins Leadership, Nashville 2023). p. 148.

www.ingramcontent.com/pod-product-compliance
Lightning Source LLC
Chambersburg PA
CBHW011846200326
41597CB00028B/4721